D0512779

CELEBRATING ADVENT

CELEBRATING ADVENT

Edited by
Robert Heyer

The articles in this book originally appeared in the *New Catholic World*, or in the *New Catholic World* or 1984 of *The Missionary Society of St. Paul the Apostle in the State of New York.*

All rights reserved. No part of this book may be reproduced or transmitted in any form or by any means, electronic or mechanical, including photocopying, recording or by any information storage and retrieval system without permission in writing from the Publisher.

Published by Paulist Press
Editorial Offices: 997 Macarthur Blvd., Mahwah, N.J. 07430
Business Offices: 545 Island Road, Ramsey, N.J. 07446

PAULIST PRESS
New York / Ramsey / Toronto

Art and Design: Gloria Ortíz

Photos: John Glaser

Library of Congress
Catalog Card Number: 74-28634

ISBN: 0-8091-1864-5

Published by Paulist Press
Editorial Office: 1865 Broadway, N.Y., N.Y. 10023
Business Office: 545 Island Rd., Ramsey, N.J. 07446

Printed and bound in the United States of America

CONTENTS

ADVENT TRADITIONS

AROUND THE WORLD

Mary Louise Tietjen

Advent is "a coming," and in reality it is *our* coming, for the Lord is always there. Advent is a miniature of the larger journey through time, just as the elaborate nativity setting of many lands is a miniature of the larger milieu. Both journeys have a beginning and an end, and the ending is always a birthday.

But the American scene, which explodes into full-scale celebration the day after Thanksgiving, is not supportive of this concept. It is difficult to realize Advent as journey, as preparation, as fast before the feast. We have instead instant Christmas all the way. And so we are cheated of the arrival. (It is possible for revelers to ride right through Bethlehem and never know it.)

Is the season better kept elsewhere? Perhaps a look at the Advent passage of other lands will help—not, heaven forbid, to impose more "things we ought to do" (however attractive), but rather to bring fresh vision to our own customs so that we can simplify, so that we can discover the one or two signs with great meaning for us, so that we can develop these consistently and well.

Such a survey, at least, has given me an image of myself; it is Lady Befana who brings gifts to Italian children on Epiphany, said to be the source of her name. Long ago she was invited by the wise men, no less, to go with them to find the child. But she would not—she was busy, the house to clean, the meals, many pressing duties. It was an inconvenient time for a trip, let alone a search. But after her distinguished guests had gone, she changed her mind and set out to catch up with the caravan. She has been traveling ever since. On the way, longer than any Advent journey, she leaves presents for the sleeping

Mary Louise Tietjen has written articles and poetry for many publications including *Religion Teacher's Journal, Living Light,* and *Today's Parish.*

children because they remind her of the one she seeks.

Surely she represents many of us Christmas Marthas, lacking the better part, full of good intentions and second thoughts. (And I believe gift-giving twelve days after Christmas would be about right. I could make it by then, just as I used to have my children completely outfitted for winter—everyone with two mittens, two boots, one snowsuit, one scarf, one earmuffs—by January thaw.)

The Advent project in many countries across the world is the setting up of the nativity scene. Americans may think of the crib as a final (and hopefully most important) feature of the Christmas home, the last of the stored and labeled boxes to be unpacked on December 24, a necessary adjunct to the tree.

Not so everywhere. The tree is secondary and sometimes not there at all. But the manger begins to take shape weeks before Christmas, for the figures are many and the settings extensive, even taking over a whole room. What will emerge is not simply a vignette of the holy land, but an entire local landscape superimposed, woven in, to become a more familiar holy land, surely one of the most endearing celebrations of the incarnate ever devised. Here each culture finds its sacred time and sacred place.

And so in the Spanish Christmas stable there will be not only the customary little gray donkey but a fine Spanish bull; approaching with the shepherds is a famous toreador, one shoulder, flaunting his cape.

The cottonwood santos of Old and New Mexico, once thought of as crude native art, are now behind glass in cathedral, village church, and city museum. Nuestra Señora is equally loved as a great lady with jeweled crown and a wardrobe for every feast day, or as a young mother in apron and reboso, kneeling before El Niño.

German cribs are fashioned by a people who seem to be natural-born wood carvers. Treasured pieces will have come perhaps from the Nuremberg Fair or the workshops of Oberammergau.

The heirloom figures of Czechoslovakia (home of the Good King Wenceslaus) were often constructed of stiff bread dough, then elaborately painted. These were family-made and added to each year, a favorite Advent occupation.

The little cribs of Poland are often shadow-boxed in wooden frames, very convenient for carrying in processions. And El Salvador is noted for its very tiny scenes, miniatures of the miniature.

In Italy, where on the Christmas Eve of 1223 St. Francis gave us the first Christmas crib, the manger is the presepio. Sometimes each child will have his different one, set up on the bottom shelf of a little open pyramid of surprises.

Ecuador's pesebre is usually arranged in the entrance hall. A blue paper background traces a Middle East skyline, but the foreground is full of Indian children costumed for their festival dance and llamas in bell and blanket, nimbly footing their way to Bethlehem.

In Provence, the clay santons of the crèche will depict, besides the Holy Family, the mayor and the judge, the village gossip with umbrella, a young wife at the spinning wheel, hunters with their dogs, gypsies always, and many, many shepherds. Older collections can trace the history of costume for a century and a half. It was a Frenchman who said, "The man who makes a santon plays God, and, like him, fashions a man from clay."

Nor is every manger a period piece, presenting just the ghosts of Christmas past. The people who originally constructed them reflected the actual life of their time; their work can live and grow. For example, a Venezuelan pesebre, with its antique pieces of delicate balsa wood, will also show the soccer team, students on motor bikes, secretaries at the typewriter, a bulldozer, an airport, and here, at the steepest incline, behold Mérida's cable car, climbing toward snowy peaks!

To supply such remarkable scenes, there were and are the famous Christmas fairs—not every family produces its own santonnier. Americans who commonly vacation in July and August seldom see these great festive anticipations. Set up in the open air, in booths and kiosks, in Indian puestos, around plaza, piazza, and city square, at Marseilles, on the cathedral steps of Barcelona, in the stalls at Oaxaca, in the heart of Rome, in the cold Tyrol and in tropical San Jose, these fairs offer enchanting toys, extraordinary edibles, and every requirement for your Christmas panorama.

In Latin America, one necessity will be colored sawdust for basic landscaping. Flat baskets of many tints, together with pine cones and soft

mosses, will be displayed at all markets south of the border.

For a realistic meadow, you will have had the foresight to plant grass in a wide pan so that your shepherd and his flock will be knee-deep in living, growing green, come Christmas eve. Pan edges are obscured by pebbled walls and bramble thickets. It becomes clear, does it not, why one of the special pleasures of the season is visiting the neighbors' Christmas scenes?

4

In our native land, where can we see something of these wonders? New Yorkers can view the superlative presepio of the Metropolitan Museum of Art where, in a center court, the tree is radiant with a Glory of 18th-century angels (and that is the proper collective noun, in every sense of the word). Surrounding the tree, at home in an intricate landscape whose many roads lead to a tender Madonna and her child, are the minstrels, the beggars, the rich city folk, the more welcome guests eating and drinking at the inhospitable inn, the magi in oriental splendor with an exotic entourage of Moors and Mongols—they carry silver scimitars designed by famous silversmiths. Here also are the lords and ladies of the Neapolitan court whose hobby it was to order, collect, and even costume themselves these very figures. All this magnificence remains in place at the Metropolitan until well after Christmas. The collection and its annual arrangement are both a Christmas gift to New York from Loretta Hines Howard.

Another renowned crib is that of the Moravian Community in Bethlehem, Pennsylvania. Here the crib is called a "putz," from putzen, meaning to clean, fix up, and decorate. And decorated it is! The large handcarved figures inhabit a land complete with running streams, waterfalls, bridges, windmills, and log cabins. It requires weeks of preparation, but it will be ready for its many pilgrims by the time the lovefeast of hot coffee and sweet bun has been served to all and the candlelit service is over on Christ-

mas eve. The great putz is echoed by smaller ones in the Moravian homes of Bethlehem, Lititz, and Winston-Salem. The construction the the crib, the baking for all comers, the pouring of innumerable beeswax candles, and the perfecting of their unequaled Christmas music—these are the Advent preparations of a dedicated people.

I have recently enjoyed an American dollhouse exhibit with furnishings exact down to the hinges and pulls on the corner cupboard. Kitchens were completely outfitted with pots and pans. Counters held pies, cakes, and a turkey glistening from the oven.

Tiny gold-framed portraits hung on the wall, and there was a needlepoint footstool. The people who occupied these dwellings were in scale: grandfather nodded in his easy chair and baby slept in her colonial cradle.

What happens to all this marvelous art of the miniature at Christmas? Must our American cribs be so unimaginative, predictable, and sparse? Is there so great a demand for these awesome doll collections, and none at all for a nativity group which would teach and delight American children for generations? (I suppose my personal dream is for a three-dimensional Lauren Ford manger, set in a New England barn.)

But there are other ways, life-size, to prepare for Christmas. One that emphasizes the Advent journey theme is the acting out of Las Posadas. In

Mexico and our southwest, for nine days before Christmas, a procession of grown-ups and children will go from house to house seeking shelter (or lodgings, the meaning of "posadas"). Sometimes the holy ones are simply small figures borne on a platform; often, actual people take their parts, and there may be a live burro. When the procession reaches a designated home, there is a sung dialogue between those outside and those inside (cf. *Make Ready the Way of the Lord* by Irene Mary Naughton, Bruce Pub. Co. Milwaukee, 1966):

Q. Will you give us shelter?
   We've no place to stay,
   We have come from Nazareth
   On the long rough way.

A. No we do not want you
   Knocking there below.
   You must be a robber,
   Get away and go!

Several exchanges follow, until at last the insiders are convinced:

This is Joseph and sweet Mary?
Banish all your gloom and sadness.
Sing the songs of happy welcome,
Ring the bells of joy and gladness!

Come in from outside our doorway.
You must be so cold and tired.
We're so happy you have come here,
Come and sit beside our fire.

And so the doors are thrown open; there will be simple refreshments for the weary ones, and perhaps a piñata for the children to break, with its shower of nuts and candy.

The drama can be shortened to fewer nights, or a family can condense it to visitations at the front and back door, but basically and originally this is a novena ending on Christmas Eve, when the procession, now with the figure of an infant, enters the church to place the child on the waiting straw.

Two customs with which we are more familiar are the Advent Wreath and the Advent calendar. Like the tree (whose ornaments are the most beautiful in the world), they come to us from Germany. Both stress the waiting and the longing of the period; they make time visible for children, one with its lighted candles for successive Sundays in Advent, the other with translucent picture windows to be opened each December day. The best description I know of the Advent Wreath tradition is given by Maria Trapp (*The Sound of Music* Maria) in *The Story of the Trapp Family Singers*, "An Austrian Christmas."
Parents will enjoy this Italian Christmas tradition. Well before the day of the bambino, each child composes a letter to father and mother, thanking them and wishing them all happiness. It is hidden under father's plate, where with great surprise he finds and reads it on Christmas Eve.

I have a 1912 letter mailed from a boarding school by my mother to her mother; it is just such a Christmas piece, full of formal good wishes. Puzzled, I asked: Wasn't she coming home for the holidays that very afternoon? Of course. But this was her Christmas letter manifesting filial de-

votion and progress in penmanship. A worthy tradition!

Two popular saints grace the Advent season and lighten the journey for us; one is St. Nicholas whose feast is December 6, and the other is St. Lucy, bright saint of the long dark Swedish winter, whose feast is December 13.

Nicholas, patron of Greece and Old Russia, name saint of pope and antipope, emperor and patriarch, was a 4th-century bishop of Myra, an important Greek seaport, now Demre, a forgotten town in Turkey with an empty tomb. But his relics are honored from his Italian shrine in Bari to St. Nicholas Church and Holy Trinity Cathedral in Manhattan. He is the special friend of sailors and children,

and in several countries, principally Holland, he is the gift-bringer. First he makes an actual appearance, with his mitre and crozier, on the eve of his feast, and then next morning the presents are found. Thoughtful children will leave hay in their shoes for his great white horse—but hope to avoid his unpleasant helper, variously known throughout Europe as Knecht Ruprecht, Black Peter, Krampus, etc. Dutch families who came to New Amsterdam brought beloved St. Nicholas and left Knecht Ruprecht at home, for which we thank them.

St. Lucy is Sicilian, the beloved Santa Lucia of Italian song. How did she get to Sweden? Long ago, it is said, she came to the aid of the northern nation in its blackest hour,

when a famine devastated the land. They have never forgotten. In a halo of lighted candles, Swedish daughters continue her role, bringing a breakfast-in-bed of coffee and saffron bun to the starving household. Today every Swedish (and Swedish-American) town, school, and office building elects its Lucia bride for her day.

Advent is the time of all the year for "baking ahead," especially in countries like Sweden where Christmas is a deep-winter feast, and an oven going in the kitchen is very pleasant. The overwhelming abundance of Christmas is not lightly achieved with one wave of a wooden spoon.

And so for the British housewife, it all begins on Stir-Up Sunday, the first in Advent, when everyone in the family is expected to lend a hand with the plum pudding, while making a Christmas wish. The standard recipe calls for a few threepenny silver coins—bite with care! Then, laced with brandy, what is affectionately known as The Pud is left to mellow till the great day.

Ireland's good mother will mix her Cake-of-the-Year as early as October or November. When it has aged, it will be given a coat of almond paste and icing one inch thick. (An old Gaelic name for Christmas is Night of Cakes.)

Christmas breads, many highly symbolic, are a subject to themselves. The christopsomo, the Christ bread of Greece, is eaten with honey on Christmas Eve. German christstollen and Czechoslovakian calta are both plaited, criss-cross, to remind of swaddling clothes. And of course the blessed wafer bread of the Slavic people (oplatek to the Poles, bread of angels to the Lithuanians) is always the first course of the vigilia feast, shared in an age-old ritual of love and thanksgiving.

Then there are the requisite fourteen kinds of Norwegian cookie; the Dutch speculatius, rich in honey and nuts; Swiss delights made in wooden picture molds; and Italian strufoli and frappe, pastry ribbons and bows, light as air, dusted with powdered sugar; and cinnamon stars and gingerbread men and lebkuchen and pfefferneusse and nurnberger daisies and zucker hutchen, those little sugar hats. Oh yes, Lord, we knew you were coming and we did indeed bake a cake!

And so at last it is Christmas Eve, that night of nights. In Spain, it is Noche Buena, with promenades and serenades after Midnight Mass, and then the cena, a late and bountiful family feast.

In Switzerland, the bells are ringing. Christmas bonfires burn on the Alps, and the smaller fires of many lanterns are following the leader down the valleys to church, a moving thread of light

In the Congo, wise men in hot-colored robes and shepherds with their goats are coming before a real baby under his thatch-roofed shelter. Tomorrow the drums will beat for the march-around offering of fruit, vegetables, and wood carvings—birthday gifts to the child.

In France, the table is set for le réveillon after Midnight Mass (and a small repast set out in case the child should come while the family is at church). But little children are in bed, shoes carefully placed so that Père Noël cannot overlook them.

In Ireland the candle is in the window. It will burn all night to welcome the child—or any stranger—as once, they say, it signaled a haven to the hunted priest of a troubled time.

The Philippines are aglow with a constellation of many-pointed star lanterns; strolling minstrels sing beneath them. The candles clustered around the crib are pink, green, blue, white, and gold.

Polish people everywhere are watching for the first star, a sign to begin the many courses of the vigilia. Their table will keep a vacant chair for the Christ Child.

In Russia, where the Christmas tree is now a New Year's tree, there will still be those, especially in the Ukraine, who on this night bless each room of the house, stand wheat sheaves in the corner, spread straw beneath the tablecloth, and light the Christ candle, held straight in a freshly baked loaf. Their Bethlehem is truly a house of bread.

In Norway, it is the Yule-peace, and an end to quarrels, ancient or current. Throughout Scandinavia, the animals have been given extra rations and told: "Eat well, keep well, this is Christmas eve!" Sheaves of grain for the birds are bound at the entrance to the house, at the country gate, and on the apartment balcony. And a saucer of cinnamon rice pudding has been set out for the household elf.

Even in Japan Santa Ojiisan is preparing for a busy night.

All over Latin America, the fireworks are cascading in the summer dark. Christmas homes are sweet-scented with jasmine and roses. Greens set with tiny tropical birds, and banks of poinsettia (that flower of the holy night) surround the crib. Later, much later, to maracas and music-sticks, the children will dance before the child. They will sing: "This is the good night, and not a night to sleep!"

There will be dancing too at Taos, at sunset, as the deer dancers lead out the procession of the Virgin. Bonfires of crossed sticks will light their way, framing the many levels of the pueblo.

Throughout the southwest, the lumin-

Suggested Readings

For those who would like to know more about the many customs of Advent and Christmas, the library stacks are full, both in the adults' and the children's sections.

There is much material in the books of Daniel J. Foley and Marguerite Ickis, prolific authorities on festival. See *Christmas the World Over, Little Saints of Christmas, The Christmas Tree, Christmas in the Good Old Days*, etc., by Daniel J. Foley, and *The Book of Religious Holidays and Celebrations, The Book of Christmas, The Book of Festival Holidays*, etc., by Marguerite Ickis.

There are also the collections edited by Herbert H. Wernecke gathering Christmas stories, essays, and reports. See his *Christmas Customs Around the World, Christmas Stories from Many Lands*, etc.

There is the recent *Book of Christmas Folklore* by the University of Pennsylvania folklorist, Tristram P. Coffin, a secular compilation garnered chiefly from Anglo-Saxon tradition, which is relatively meager.

A good summary is included in *Celebrations—The Complete Book of American Holidays* by Robert J. Myers. It has a five-page bibliography on festival, many titles solely related to Christmas.

From these you can learn everything from the proper costume for a starboy to a simple way to prepare the boar's head for the feast.

Perhaps the most useful source is still *The Christmas Book* by Francis X. Weiser, a frequent reference in later surveys, and a loving and well-documented handbook.

arias are blooming. Mountain passes, desert towns, San Xavier del Bac, the university campus, the plaza at Santa Fe, Old Town in Albuquerque, adobe homes with a chili string at the door and a piñon fire in each corner fireplace—all are rimmed and outlined by the soft flicker of thousands upon thousands of candles in their little brown bags, the color of earth, as if the earth, this night, caught fire.

And everywhere the little saints of the manger scenes, the Christmas gardens, crèches, krippes, belens, portals, nacimientos, portals, and pesebres, are expecting one more who will fill a central space: a holy people who await the presence of their king.

In Bethlehem, in the Church of the Nativity, with the filigree lamps swinging and the incense rising, the child is gently placed upon a great silver star in the grotto floor, then laid to rest in a rock-hewn niche in the wall. In my end is my beginning.

How wonderful is your name, O Lord, over all the earth!

MARANATHA

Jean Marie Hiesberger

John Glaser

John Glaser is a member of the theology department at the University of Detroit, and has published articles in *Theological Studies* and *Commonweal*.

Jean Marie Heisberger is an associate editor for Paulist Press and general editor of the *Come To The Father* series.

Then, in the sixth month, the angel Gabriel was sent from God to a Galilean town, Nazareth by name, to a young woman who was engaged to a man called Joseph (a descendant of David). The girl's name was Mary. The angel entered her room and said,

"Greetings to you, Mary. O favored one!—the Lord is with you!"

Mary was deeply perturbed at these words and wondered what such a greeting could possibly mean. But the angel said to her,

"Do not be afraid, Mary; God loves you dearly. You are going to be the mother of a son, and you will call him Jesus. He will be great and will be known as the Son of the Most High. The Lord God will give him the throne of his forefather, David, and he will be king over the people of Jacob forever. His reign shall never end."
Luke 1:26-38

"There will be signs in the sun and moon and stars, and on the earth there will be dismay among the nations and bewilderment at the roar of the surging sea. Men's courage will fail completely as they realize what is threatening the world, for the very powers of heaven will be shaken.

Then men will see the Son of Man coming on a cloud with great power and splendour! But when these things begin to happen, stand up, hold your heads high, for you will soon be free."

Luke 21:25-33

The night is nearly over, the day has almost dawned.

Romans 13:12

I lift up my eyes toward the mountains;
  whence shall help come to me?
My help is from the Lord,
  who made heaven and earth.
May he not suffer your foot to slip;

  may he slumber not who guards you:
Indeed he neither slumbers nor sleeps,
  the guardian of Israel.
The Lord is your guardian; the Lord is your shade;
  he is beside you at your right hand.
The sun shall not harm you by day,
  nor the moon by night.
The Lord will guard you from all evil;
  he will guard your life.
The Lord will guard your coming and your going,
  both now and forever.

Psalm 121

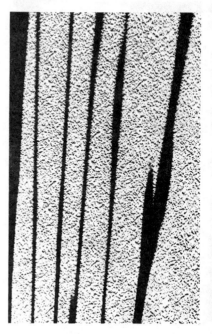

With little delay Mary got ready and hurried off to the hillside town in Judea where Zachariah and Elizabeth lived. She went into their house and greeted Elizabeth. When she heard Mary's greeting, the unborn child stirred inside her and she herself was filled with the Holy Spirit, and cried out,

"Blessed are you among women,/and blessed is your child!/What an honor it is to have the mother of my Lord/ come to see me!/As soon as your greeting reached my ears,/the child within me jumped for joy!/Oh, how happy is the woman who believes in God,/for his promises to her come true."
Luke 1:39-46

The voice of one crying in the wilderness,
Make ye ready the way of the Lord,
Make his paths straight.
Every valley shall be filled,
And every mountain and hill shall be brought low:
And the crooked shall become straight,
And the rough ways smooth:
And all flesh shall see the salvation of God.
Isaiah 40:3-5

Jesus gave them this reply, "Go and tell John what you hear and see—that blind men are recovering their sight, cripples are walking, lepers being healed, the deaf hearing, the dead being raised to life and the good news is being given to those in need. And happy is the man who never loses his faith in me."
Matthew 11:3ff.

14

How lovely is your dwelling place,
  O Lord of hosts!
My soul yearns and pines
  for the courts of the Lord.
My heart and my flesh
  cry out for the living God.
Even the sparrow finds a home,
  and the swallow a nest
  in which she puts her young—
Your altars, O Lord of hosts,
  my king and my God!
Happy they who dwell in your house!
  continually they praise you.

Psalm 84

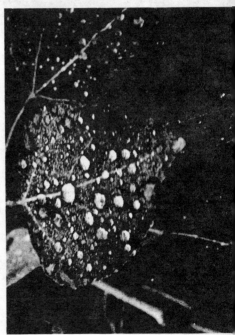

The birth of Jesus Christ happened like this. When Mary was engaged to Joseph, before their marriage, she was discovered to be pregnant—by the Holy Spirit. Whereupon Joseph, her future husband, who was a good man and did not want to see her disgraced, planned to break off the engagement quietly. But while he was turning the matter over in his mind an angel of the Lord appeared to him in a dream and said, "Joseph, son of David, do not be afraid to take Mary as your wife! What she has conceived is conceived through the Holy Spirit, and she will give birth to a son, whom you will call Jesus ('the Savior') for it is he who will save his people from their sins."

Matthew 1:18-21

WAITING

John Gallen

Has it ever impressed you that many of the folks sitting around you in the "waiting room" of an air terminal or bus depot don't really appear to be "waiting" at all? They betray no signs, often enough, of expectation, of alert watching for something to happen. They seem bored. Uninterested. Even sleepy and asleep. Oh, there are exceptions to this unexciting pattern of non-activity, to be sure, but surely you've seen the type —people whose apparent lack of interest in what's happening or about to happen makes them seem out of place in a "waiting" room.

Or perhaps you've been frustrated by the "wait-er" or "wait-ress" whose ti-

John Gallen, S.J., Director of the Murphy Center for Liturgical Research, is an eminent liturgist and lecturer.

tle belies the facts of the scene: no compassion for the moanings of hunger evidenced by patrons on all sides!

Instead of paying attention to the melancholy plight of would-be diners, an all-absorbing conversation with another employee wins out over all distress signals from those who are fainting away! Not really "one-who-waits," one who is alert to help, ready to minister, sensitive to need. Not really a "wait-er."

Even the most important places and events of our human lives can be lost on us. If, for example, we are to believe Dr. Frederick Leboyer, we don't know how to "wait on" the needs and desires of the struggling infant engaged in the process of childbirth. Dr. Leboyer's new book, *Birth Without Violence,* now taking the country by storm, makes a list of parent-doctor-nurse insensitivities that are ter-

17

rifying in their implications. Bright lamps and floodlights in delivery rooms that simply blind the infant; loud talking that makes him cringe in fear; slapping and spanking that produces (especially when upside down) not proud demonstrations of vigor but sobs of anguish! "Speak the language of lovers," is the doctor's advice. "And what is the essential language of lovers? No speech. Touch. Lovers are shy, modest. When they want to embrace, they seek the darkness; they turn out the light. Or simply close their eyes. They create night for themselves. Touch becomes everything" (p. 36). A scene of sensitive alertness. Of paying attention. Of waiting on another. Of watching. Vigil.

Reading Leboyer's book made me reflect on the whole wide range of insensitivity that colors our lives together. Times I don't "wait on" the needs that are crying out within me, when I don't keep vigil before the searchings of those who surround me and share similar hungers and thirst, endless sleepiness without expectation that something's about to happen—or excitement that something's already happening. Babies in childbirth are not the solitary victims of inattention or cruelly presumptive treatment.

The Christian experience makes professional "wait-ers" out of us. Followers of Jesus are those who are waiting on Jesus. They keep watch for the moment when he will be finally and astonishingly manifest, speaking the language of lovers, holding the dominion of Lord. "Now we watch for the day, hoping that the salvation promised us will be ours when Christ our Lord will come again in his glory." That is the Advent prayer of the Church (Preface of Advent I). In Advent we see ourselves in our attitude of watching and waiting. "I am listening. What is the Lord saying?" (Ps. 85:8). Listen. Watch. Wait. Be silent! Advent is the time of silence when we wait upon the coming of the Lord. Not his coming at Bethlehem. That is already our treasure, and he is already with us. It isn't that we forget or disregard Bethlehem. The gift of Bethlehem draws the focus of our waiting beyond that small town to the gift of his brimming presence about to be shown in all its transfiguring fullness. "Come, Lord Jesus!"

Simone Weil wrote in her mystic way that "the effort that brings a soul to salvation is like the effort of looking or of listening; it is the kind of effort by which a fiancée accepts her lover. It is an act of attention and consent, whereas what language designates as will is something suggestive of muscular effort," she pointed out in the collection of letters and essays entitled *Waiting for God* (p. 193). Advent has a very special way of clarifying the dynamics of our relationship with the God of mystery who "dwells in unapproachable light." The dynamics come to this: experience of God occurs and flowers only when the God who aboundingly transcends every form of human experience and human imagining uncovers himself to us. He can't be grasped or bullied or pressured or pushed into showing himself. That is the kind of "muscular effort" to which Weil alludes. (Interestingly, Dag Hammarskjold parodied the same radically futile effort, calling it "muscular heroism" in *Markings*, p. 67.) We need to wait on God, not attempt (however fruitlessly) to program him or entrap him. Advent shapes our prayer as a prayer of waiting. "Now we watch for the day."

God is not vague. In all his holiness, he is beyond. Far from being a mere puzzle to tax the wits and cleverness of human persons, he escapes utterly whatever energies we can muster to comprehend his sacred reality. He is hidden. "Truly, thou art a God who hidest thyself" (Is. 45:15). He cannot be touched. "If God is hidden," Abhishiktananda writes, "it is because he is out of the reach of our senses or imagination, even of our mental perceptions. God and the world do not form a unity within the grasp of thought, as was generally supposed by the Greek philosophers—a belief which would reduce him to an object within the range of our minds" (*Prayer*, p. 9). Perhaps because we have become so immune to surprise all around us and within us as well, God is no surprise to us. And so we move close to the presumption of surrounding his reality within the dimensions of human expectation. We find God as predictable as our friend, and are sadly twice mistaken. But Advent inspires a prayer of surprise and genuine expectation: "Our hearts desire the warmth of your love and our minds are searching for the light of

your Word," is the Opening Prayer for the First Sunday. And it goes further: "Increase our longing!" There is no muscular religion here. Only waiting. Only vigil.

The fourteenth-century author of *The Cloud of Unknowing* cautioned his readers about the mystery that is God in this way: "Though we cannot know him we can love him. By love he may be touched and embraced, never by thought." It is the embrace of love that is definitive. So "let God awaken your longing and draw you to himself in this cloud while you strive with the help of his grace to forget everything else." Knowledge, for all of its import, pales and is humiliated by its own radical impotence. And love itself is not of our doing, but of God's doing. Our hearts leap up in his presence only when he shows us his presence. We wait upon him, and watch for the day when he will reveal himself utterly. At the manifestation of his presence, we are "still as a stone" (Ex.15:16).

This adoring silence, whether it is physical or not (and it often is), characterizes the Advent prayer of the "waiting world" (Opening Prayer of the Second Sunday). The world waits. Waiting becomes our ideal in Advent: "May he find us waiting." "Grant that we may be ready to receive Christ." "Help us who wait for his coming." "Help us to look forward." "Guide us with your love as we await the coming." "We keep vigil for the dawn of salvation." These are the controlling sentiments of the liturgy's prayer during Advent.

But there is a trap in all this. "It is good that one should wait quietly for the salvation of the Lord," says Lamentations (3:26). And so Zephaniah counsels: "Be silent before the Lord God" (1:7). The advice is, of course, crucial to any authentic religious experience, but it is open to profound misunderstanding. It is possible to interpret this necessary silence before God, this "waiting," as something which men and women can engineer in a non-divine (i.e., "merely human") way, as the predisposing of the human heart for divine action. Nothing could be further from the truth! The silence itself is God's work. The waiting, the expectancy, the restlessness, and the very desire for God are his gracious gift. "The Lord God has opened my ear," Isaiah proclaimed (50:5). If one is to be sensitive to his presence, to his coming, it will only be because the Lord himself renders one sensitive. There is no desire for God except the desire that the Lord himself implants and fosters in one's heart.

Desire is an important word to describe waiting. True desire is a consuming experience. The person who is enflamed by desire has all his energies and powers roar with a compelling and relentless demand. There is no sleeping, except what exhaustion forces. Only vigil. Standing watch. Anticipation. Desire is a craving that will not accept frustration or denial. The desire for God is itself God's gift. Waiting for God is itself the beginning of true experience of his presence because it is his creative impulse in our hearts. The liturgy of Advent is trying to release all those energies of desire which burn within us. It seeks to give them vent. "Open our hearts in welcome to prepare for the coming of our Savior": the very preparation, the very welcome, is God's gracious touch upon us (December 20).

There is another word that is inextricably entwined within the fabric of the Advent experience, to which we must now turn. It is another word of waiting: hope! It would be difficult for many persons to characterize our moment of history in America today as an age that is filled with hope. And there are reasons that weigh heavily, aren't there, in the shaping of such a pessimistic evaluation? Early each day, the commentator on one of the nation's morning news programs begins his broadcast by saying: "Good morning. Here's what's happening." And then he begins to relate, item by item, a list of events that may well produce pessimism in us: Irishmen blow up Irishmen, Vietnamese behead other Viet-

namese, Americans betray their comrades, husbands desert families, wives stab husbands, lovers trifle with love, children have their emotional lives unstrung as they are relentlessly beset by the crushing problems that pitilessly afflict their parents. Here's what's happening, indeed! The racial wars, the generation wars, the sexual wars, the political wars, the personal wars, and the economic wars career along their explosive and deadly ways, devastating life and laughter, beauty, peace, harmony, love, and, so very pervasively, hope! But Advent is about hopeful waiting. Does a list of our sufferings, or a catalogue of our sins, eviscerate the possibilities of Advent for us?

If hope means "to expect the best to happen," not just to reason or think that it is likely, but to *expect* it to happen, then one must conclude that very many men and women of our age find themselves, they say, incapable of it. They are unable to hope.

"Just look around," they will tell you, "look around at the misery!" The idea of hope becomes laughable. "To expect the best, in the midst of this!" In one parish of this country recently, one of the young Jesuits who works there told me about the four funerals that took place during one week of the past summer: there were three murders, and one suicide. Hope?

Yet there are some words of challenge for the Christian community of waiting to be found in the First Letter of Peter (3:15): "Have your answer ready for people who ask you the reason for the hope that you all have." What hope is that? Holy Scripture describes us as a people of hope! Are we? Can we be, as we examine the devastation that has been worked in our world and history and, in a measure which each of us knows, in our own lives?

Hope is about the future. To hope for something is to wait confidently, to look forward confidently to the future when you *expect* something to happen. Now, clearly, there is a daydreaming way of talking about hope which is not the genuine experience: "I 'hope' that I'll inherit a million dollars tomorrow so I can pay all my bills and leave on a fabulous vacation," or, "I 'hope' I'll be named President of this country by acclamation, so that I'll really be able to take charge of all our problems here at home and, at the same time, straighten out the international situation." Daydreaming. But authentic hope is something else. What makes the difference? Real hope is based on something, founded in something solid and real. True hope for the future is based on the present. What already is present, now, provides a glimpse, however dimly, of what may be expected to fill the future.

So there we are! That is what the liturgy of Advent forces us to. If Advent is about expectant hope, about waiting with confidence for the future, on what is our hope founded? What validates the Advent liturgy, the Advent experience? What makes it authentic and real? In other words: what do we have in our *present,* now, that provides a reason to hope for the best in the *future?* Hope is about *promises.* A hope is a promise for the future. Advent is a liturgy of hope for a "waiting world." What is there in your life and my life which you and I can count as a promise for the future? "Have your answer ready for people who ask you the reason for the hope that you all have."

Advent is a prayer of hope for the future coming of the Lord that is based upon the reality of our experience of his presence now, here, in our midst, with us. Emmanuel. If we are an Advent people of hope, it is because we already know his presence, feel his touch upon us. "My soul rejoices in my God" (Third Sunday). Present joy opens out the promise for future joy: "Shout for joy, daughter of Zion; Israel, shout aloud! The Lord your God is in your midst, a victorious warrior. He will exult with joy over you, he will renew you by his love; he will dance with shouts of joy for you as on a day of festival" (Third Sunday).

The encounter with presence. Where? The meeting with the God of mystery. Where does it take place? What is the locus of our encounter with the Holy One? It is in every outpouring that rises from the creative depths of the Creator Lord. Everything of our world and cosmos is the gift of his

presence, delicately nuanced in shape and beauty to hold the shining mystery of God. We ourselves, other persons, our world—it is all the outpouring of God.

There were some old-fashioned "spiritualities" which offered us a pair of unrealistic options in the matter of religious experience. One mode of spirituality theorized that, in the encounter with another creature, I do not really encounter that creature so much as this meeting is the occasion for my meeting with God (thus one could say, for example, that he loved another person simply "for the sake of God" and not at all for himself). Another and opposite theory expressed itself this way: When I meet another creature, that is the extent of the encounter. I do not meet God in this meeting with creation, though I may allude to his existence (often this was "taking it on faith"). Two views of the human person's experience of creation: one bypasses creation for the Creator; the other halts at creation, ignorant (even agnostic) about the Creator.

But it is not so, and we need not be forced to a choice between these unlikely options. For in every genuine encounter with created reality, there is an experience of two realities: created reality and its life-giving font, created mystery and holy mystery that is its source. The reality in which we are immersed is the embrace of God, for "ever since the creation of the world his invisible nature, namely, his eternal power and deity, has been clearly perceived in the things

that have been made" (Rom. 1:20). We are plunged into the great sea of holy mystery which engulfs us in its own sacred reality.

But creation is not a thing. It is an event. Creation is that event in which divine mystery shares its own splendor by giving expression to itself in us and the cosmic reality that is the arena of our life and activity. And so

we cry out, "The earth is the Lord's and the fullness thereof, the world and those who dwell therein" (Ps. 24:1). Looking about at what he was doing in the creative event that gave beginning to the history that we share together, "God saw everything that he had made, and behold, it was very good" (Gen. 1:31). As the shadowy sign of holy mystery, creation is holy and mysterious, sacred and life-giving. Profanity rises not from sacred reality but from the ambiguity of our response to it, whether by manipulating it or by despising it and so failing to reverence the sacred mystery of creation which discloses the mystery of God himself. But it is no less sacred for all of that. It remains the expressive shining-forth of the *mysterium tremendum et fascinans.*

We observed earlier that all authentic religious experience begins with God, with what God does. So, the divine creation-event is the beginning of religious experience. The communication of God is the fecund word of creation which is uttered by holy mystery: "For he spoke, and it came to be; he commanded, and it stood forth" (Ps. 33:9). God's creative Word, shaping the very pattern of our being, begins the dialogue of faith and religious experience, the dialogue of prayer.

Advent liturgy is rooted in the fact that all creation is patterned upon and has come to its fullness in the manifestation of God in Jesus. Advent liturgy is expectant: it waits for the Lord to come again, and prays in hope for a future. That hope is founded, not in theory but in experience. It is founded in the experience of real presence! The experience of Christian men and women has been and is that holy creation is the image of Jesus the Lord, the sacrament of God. God is already with us, so we have hope for a future!

How do you know? How can you tell if there is reason to hope? Can you celebrate Advent as "worship in spirit and in truth"? Is there any way of knowing that the misery which we endure, and have in part created, is not the *only* real thing in our lives? Is there anything holy in my life now, in the present, that promises a future

with God? If I am alive, now, in the mystery of God, then I have something to hope in, look forward to, expect to happen: the experience of becoming more and more alive as I am plunged more and more deeply into the holy mystery who is my life.

What are the signs that God holds me in his life *now*? St. Paul made a list of them: signs of the presence. They are: love, joy, peace, patience, kindness, goodness, faithfulness, gentleness, self-control. If there is anything of these realities in your life, then that is God present in your life!

God is with you, making you alive now, and calling you into his future. If there is anything of authentic love, or faithfulness, then rest in that, for you rest in God! Be excited by that, for it is God who excites you! Live in that, for it is God who makes you live! These experiences of God's presence now, in our present, are the pledge of our future together and the heart of our Advent waiting in joyful and blessed hope. Our hearts are on fire for the future that is to be because they are filled with the delight of what already is. Immersed in this divine milieu, we watch for the day when our salvation will appear. Though anguished by our miserable sinfulness, we can persist in our limping fidelity, "so that when he comes he may find us watching in prayer, our hearts filled with wonder and praise." Already!

How to Celebrate Advent in the Parish

Charles W. Gusmer

Advent is not only a period of preparation for Christmas and Epiphany, it is also an occasion to seize upon the heightened motivation of this season in order to improve the quality of parish worship. The General Instruction to the Revised Order of Mass (#73, 313) assumes there will be some collaborative effort at planning and preparing the liturgy. Given the indispensable cooperation from the rectory and the necessary education—reading the introductions to

Charles Gusmer is professor of sacramental theology and liturgy at the Darlington School of Theology. He has taped a series of lectures on *The Anointing of the Sick* available from National Catholic Reporter, and has published articles in *Worship* and other magazines.

the revised rites is a good start—one common mistake of many parish liturgy teams is to move so quickly into the specifics of a particular service as to lose the forest for the trees. A remedy to this is to begin with a wide-angle vision which looks at the total worship life of the parish.

PEOPLE WHO CELEBRATE

At a recent meeting of a diocesan liturgical commission one of the lay members asserted that the biggest single problem with Sunday Mass is that the people do not clearly know why they are there. Maybe a good way to begin would be an intensified effort at identifying the reason for Sunday Mass: not a dreary obligation to be accomplished in an individualistic manner, but rather the coming together of the parish community assembled for corporate worship to remember the Lord as he asked to be remembered on Sunday, the little Easter, the first day of the week when Jesus rose from the dead. This is what makes us Church; this is how we are most Church. All of this presumes a sense of faith community among the worshipers. Is there a feeling of belongingness and committedness apart from the liturgy during the week? Is the people's participation joyous and full? Is there an atmosphere of prayerful celebration facilitated by the skillful use of music? A well-done reverent and festive celebration is always the best catechesis of any sacrament.

Within the body of Christ there are further ministries of worship that deserve attention. Perhaps at the outset of the post-Vatican liturgical renewal we were so intent upon doing the right thing that the mere implementation often took precedence over quality. Regretfully, we realize now that no true service is rendered to God or his people by tolerating sloppy servers, inarticulate readers, or, for that matter, incompetent celebrants. Urgently needed are well-trained, well-prepared ministers who not only arrive on time but also and especially are imbued with a spirituality of the ministry they fulfill (cf. General Instruction to Revised Order of Mass, Ch. III: "Offices and Ministries"). Here are some of these ministries:

Priest—the leader of prayer, the facilitator at worship who coordinates the other ministries. Then as now the priest-celebrant still remains the most important single ministry. Advent is good time to brush up on the style of presidential leadership.

Deacon—a kind of intermediary between the priest and people at worship, a knowledgeable master of ceremonies.

Acolytes/Special Eucharistic Ministers—these should be chosen with particular regard for their ministry to the sick, bringing Communion to shut-ins from the Sunday Eucharist.

Servers—why do we continue to use almost exclusively small boys for this ministry?·Why not members of both sexes with no particular designation of age, e.g., special eucharistic ministers?

Reader—the proclamation of the Word of God is too important to be poorly done. The people's continued obsession with missalettes is undoubtedly due to the generally impoverished level of scriptural proclamation. As for comments, in most cases these are unnecessary and superfluous. The liturgy already suffers from too many words and the tendency to overexplain everything empties the liturgy of all its symbolic content.

Ministries of Music—despite rumors to the contrary, choirs are needed more than ever to encourage liturgical participation. In addition to the or-

Ushers—this most stereotyped of all ministries should include personable men and women who could greet the people and help build up the parish community.

Albeit Advent-Christmas is often the busiest time of the year, nonetheless the season would be an excellent chance to schedule early enough in advance a meeting of the various ministries both to show the parish's appreciation and to update the skills and motivation of those involved. We get what we deserve. By insisting on excellence in the service of the Lord on the part of all the ministers, it will gradually evolve.

TOTAL ENVIRONMENT

Some time ago while visiting a Congregationalist building in Vermont, I asked if the particular building was the church. The lady in charge gently reminded me that the church was the people; the building is where the community gathers for worship.

Correspondingly, does the spatial environment meet the needs of the worshiping assembly? The three focal points of the sanctuary or presbytery should be the altar (central position, proper lighting, uncluttered), the lectern (only one necessary, similarly only one lectionary), and presidential chair to facilitate the president's leadership role. Ideally the choir and organ should be located near the sanctuary so that the ministers of music may be seen as well as heard. The people's seating in the future will

ganist, the ministry of music also includes other qualified instrumentalists. Furthermore, it is difficult to see how any parish worship program can be complete without a leader of song who actively leads the people and sings the antiphonal parts.

no doubt be more flexible so as to foster greater mobility and different spatial settings. According to recent Roman directives, the tabernacle or place of eucharistic reservation is best solved by a chapel apart from the main body of the church. And what about oft-neglected liturgical appointments such as the microphone system, participation aids (their principal value is the musical selections), and the parish bulletins (must we have a monopoly on ugliness?).

EVALUATION OF PRESENT LITURGICAL SERVICES

Before planning any more liturgies, sit down and evaluate what is already there. Is the scheduling of Sunday Mass appropriate, not just in terms of convenience for attending Mass at any hour, but so as to foster a coming together of the liturgical assembly on the day of the Lord? Is there a diversified format adapted to the time of celebration and the needs of those usually participating? Further questions such as these might be asked: When are baptisms celebrated? Is there a pre-baptismal preparation program for parents? How would we evaluate the last confirmation? What is the parish doing by way of preliminary catechesis for the revised rite of penance/reconciliation? Has there been a communal anointing of the sick—especially appropriate during the Advent-Christmas season—celebrated responsibly with the necessary prior preparation and follow-up care afterward? What do you do for daily Mass? How could weddings and funerals be improved

upon? Special care should be given to other liturgical services. The people's legitimate craving for non-eucharistic liturgies of corporate prayer, earlier expressed in novenas and devotions, today seemingly finds no outlet. Seasonal services, prayer groups, and the revised Liturgy of the Hours (formerly the Divine Office) could fill a much needed gap here. Advent could also be a time to solicit the feedback of the entire parish on its worship life by means of a well-formulated questionnaire.

SPECIFICS OF PLANNING

What is often the first enterprise undertaken by a nascent liturgical committee should only be embarked upon after the preliminary wide-angle vision outlined above has been given sufficient attention.

The question of *theme* is an issue which unfortunately engages too much of the energies of most planners of liturgy. A more fruitful avenue might be to provide feedback and to suggest ideas to the homilist for his sermons. At most a theme is implicit and subtle, drawn from the season of the year (e.g., Advent) or the readings (thematic correspondence of the Old Testament and Gospel readings). Above all, avoid didacticism. At times the norm for liturgy seems to be more the classroom lecture than an act of worship. The liturgy is not a teaching machine, but, as Aidan Kavanagh advises us, the liturgy teaches us as all ritual teaches—experientially, non-discursively, ambiguously, elementally.

The biggest option of all in planning the liturgy is the selection of *music and song*. Consider the value of instrumental preludes which set the mood for the celebration as the people arrive. Avoid the four-hymn syndrome (entrance, offertory, communion, recessional). First of all, these are not the most important places to sing; the responsorial psalm, the alleluia (to be sung or omitted) and the eucharistic acclamations (sanctus, memorial acclamation, great amen) are. Secondly, there is more to liturgical music than metric hymns. Antiphonal music with a cantor/leader of song is both easy to learn and particularly appropriate for psalmody and at communion.

The fact that most people can scarcely remember what they prayed for in the General Intercessions is at least one disconcerting indication that these are often wanting both in content and execution. Avoid canned petitions slavishly copied from paradigms printed a year in advance. Make up your own and try as far as possible to draw these out from the people. They should reflect the concrete vivid imagery of the proclaimed Scripture of the day as well as an awareness of the needs of the world in which we live. The General Intercessions are an opportunity for the parish community to transcend itself by praying for the needs of the universal Church, for public authorities and the salvation of nations, for those suffering particular afflictions, and finally for the local community (cf. the suggested sequence of intentions in the General Instruction, #46).

Most of all, the intercessions are prayer—not teaching or a rehash of the homily—and their execution should be interspersed with timely pauses of silence lest they succumb to the mechanical repetition to which litanic prayer is so easily susceptible.

A final concern in planning a given liturgy should be the attention shown to the *non-verbal* features. This neglect is exemplified by the fact that virtually all liturgical planning formats seldom include ceremonial directions. The texts are there but where are the actions? Yet we celebrate eucharistic meals with bread and wine; we apply blessed oil to those being initiated into the faith, ordained to ministry or who are ill; we immerse candidates for baptism in a bath of water. We use fire/light and the aromatic incense. We stand, kneel, sit, bow, and genuflect. We sign ourselves with the cross of salvation; we extend our arms in prayer; we exchange the embrace of peace. We move from place to place in procession, and, given the right circumstances, we even dance for the Lord. The most important members of any parish liturgy team are often the resource people such as artists who can constantly demonstrate to us what liturgy is more than words.

ADVENT

The revised Roman Calendar (#39) has this to say about Advent: "The season of Advent has a twofold character. It is a time of preparation for Christmas when the first coming of God's Son to men is recalled. It is also a season when minds are directed by this memorial to Christ's second coming at the end of time. It is thus a season of joyful and spiritual expectation."

The first two Sundays of Advent look toward the second coming of Christ; the last two highlight his first coming at Bethlehem. What follows are some ideas in outline form, an appropriate practice for the week, and a corresponding symbolic action to accentuate during each of the four Sundays of Advent.

First Sunday of Advent

Idea: The Christian Vision of the Future

The readings which treat of Christ's second coming afford an opportunity to develop the meaning of eschatology: not a privatization or spiritualization of the last things, but rather a corporate transformation of the entire created cosmos at the end of time, the parousia. Christianity is at the same time the most realistic and hopeful of all world religions. Christianity is the most realistic and brutally honest in its assessment of human suffering and the inevitability of death. Yet it is the most hopeful of religions when it responds to the basic human intuition that there must be more. The present experience of human suffering and death is a cosmic consequence of sin in the world: man's misuse of freedom which has

31

brought disharmony into a world that was created good. Our hope is grounded in Jesus Christ, the new head of the human race, whose death and resurrection has ushered in the last times and already begun the ultimate restoration. In the Advent season we celebrate this beginning: the Word was made flesh (Christmas); the flesh is to be glorified (Easter).

Practice:

To celebrate Advent means to prepare for Christmas. Discuss with the family how you can do this together so as to uncover the Christian meaning of the feast so often obscured by the secular materialistic trappings. Consult *The Alternate Christmas Catalogue* (P.O. Box 20626, Greensboro, N.C. 27420, $2.50) for ideas on making gifts and Christmas cards, projects which support the environment, "gift certificates" to worthy struggling causes. Live more simply and try to be more generally available to one another.

Symbol: Fire/Light

The early Church's choice of December 25th as the feast of the incarnation was an appropriation of the birthdate of the invincible sun: Christ is the new rising sun from the East. At the beginning of Mass or after the liturgy of the Word the first candle of the Advent Wreath could be lighted from the paschal candle to show the connection between Christmas and Easter. So as not to reduplicate the symbols, have no other lighted candles. Urge the people to construct their own Advent Wreath and to light it during the week in an atmosphere of shared prayer and expectation.

Second Sunday of Advent

Idea: Preparing the Way

Although Advent is not properly a penitential season, the Gospel of John the Baptizer's call to repentance is an ever-valid reminder of the need for ongoing conversion and a change of heart that profoundly marks Christian life. This is a chance to provide some preliminary catechesis on the revised rites of adult initiation and penance, as well as to use one of the new eucharistic prayers of reconciliation. What is there in our hearts which keeps us from fully accepting the Messiah? How can we prepare the way?

Practice:

Already in 1966 a statement of the National Conference of Catholic Bishops on the penitential observance of the liturgical year contained this timely advice: "Let us witness to our love and imitation of Christ by special solicitude for the sick, the poor, the underprivileged, the imprisoned, the bed-ridden, the discouraged, the stranger, the lonely, and persons of other color, nationalities or background than our own."

A more recent statement on the World Food Crisis (November 21, 1974) could well be implemented at this time by becoming better informed about this complex issue, by pressing for a legislative reform of priorities, and by fasting two days a week and giving the money saved to the poor and hungry.

Symbol: Water

The rite of blessing and sprinkling with holy water from the revised sacramentary could be celebrated during the introductory rites or in a more expanded manner after the liturgy of the Word. This is a baptismal reminder especially fitting when John the Baptist is the subject of the Gospel narrative.

Third Sunday of Advent

Idea: The Human Condition Is Where Christianity Happens

Christmas is essentially the celebration of the humanity of the Son of God. Do we take seriously the human dimension of Christianity: of Christ, the Church, ourselves? Some people are concerned about a possible denial of the divinity of Christ. Is not a much more subtle danger a denial of his humanity by considering him immune from human doubts and struggles? This is not the same Jesus we encounter in the New Testament. Or again, there is at times a tendency to regard the meaning of the resurrection as Jesus' divesting of his human nature and returning to the Father, rather than what this mystery of faith really means: the glorification of Christ as man. What about the human dimension of the Church?

It is easier to believe in a divinely founded institution rather than to also accept a community consisting of ourselves whose human condition in a time of reform with the concomitant frailty and sinfulness becomes increasingly embarrassing. And what about the human dimension of our own spirituality? Is Christianity for us a pre-fabricated spirituality superimposed on life and reality, or is it rather a making explicit, an identification of the promptings of divine grace at the core of our being?

Practice:

This week concentrate on the family as a school for holiness: the mutual support and overcoming of inevitable conflicts is where humanity and Christianity happen. Families could develop the habit of preparing for the Sunday liturgy by familiarizing themselves with the scriptural readings and using them as a basis for shared reflection and prayer.

Symbol: Human Body

The whole person worships: body and soul, mind and will, memory, imagination, emotions. Maybe involve the entire congregation in a procession. Stand during the eucharistic prayer. Bow at the appropriate times. Extend the arms in prayer at the Lord's Prayer.

Fourth Sunday of Advent

Idea: The Giving of Gifts

The reason we exchange gifts at Christmas is in imitation of the divine generosity of the Father who has given us the gift of a Savior in the power of the Holy Spirit. By way of immediate preparation for Christmas, dispose the people for the celebration of Christmas day and its liturgy by a brief catechesis.

Practice:

Take some time to be quiet, to be still, to reflect prayerfully upon the significance of Christmas.

Symbol: Gifts

While not wishing to overdo the preparation of gifts at the expense of the more important eucharistic prayer, today would be an occasion to present very concrete gifts for the poor together with the sacramental offerings of bread and wine. Also bake bread of a more substantial texture (cf. General Instruction, #283) and administer Communion under both kinds.

Other Suggestions for Advent

Provide for refreshments after Sunday Mass or plan an occasional potluck supper so as to foster a sense of Christian community among the haps pantomime, dramatization. Explore the possibility of liturgical dance during the Advent-Christmas season. Design banners to be carried in procession which pictorially represent the Advent "O Antiphons." Use audio-visual materials to enrich the liturgy or to illustrate a homily. Develop a well-rounded life of corporate worship with services such as the following: Marian devotions which would be particularly appropriate in view of the somemnity of the immaculate conception and the role of parishioners who can thereby come to know one another. Dramatize one or more of the scriptural readings: either by assigning different parts as with the passion narrative in Holy Week or by a more elaborate, perhaps Mary in Advent; a communal celebration of the revised sacrament of penance; a Christian adaptation of the feast of lights, Chanukah, which is celebrated by our Jewish brothers and sisters this time of the year (cf. *Liturgy,* Vol. 17/8 (Oct. 1972), p. 10); a children's liturgy in honor of St. Nicholas (Dec. 6), the original Santa Claus; and, best of all, a festive celebration of morning or evening prayer from the revised Liturgy of the Hours adapted for communal celebration.

he eschatological moment. Music, too, with its strong associative power, tends to be more traditional than ever around Christmas time, with carols of high and low quality, both ancient and modern, celebrating Bethlehem, shepherds, mangers and magi. Woe betide the music director (to say nothing of the manipulators of Muzak) who would venture to neglect these nostalgic themes.

The more sophisticated among us look back to a richer inheritance of Christmastide music. Some recall with relish and regret such haunting melodies as the Gregorian Chant introit for Midnight Mass, the communion versicle, and other monophonic gems of the Christmas liturgy. Advent, too, is rich in Gregorian melodies, some still used, most regrettably forgotten. Many years of experience in liturgical music convince me that a true peak of Western music, refined

C. J. McNaspy, S.J., noted writer and commentator, is a professor at Loyola University in New Orleans.

Singing the O Antiphons

C.J. McNaspy

While Advent is evocative more of hope than of nostalgia, most of us find it hard not to look backward toward the first coming. Somehow Bethlehem, in the Christian imagination, is easier to conjure up than is yet easily appreciated, is the chant associated with the "O Antiphons."

It is a commonplace that Gregorian Chant sings better in Latin than in English or most other vernaculars. Even so, when a real effort is made to adapt English to the chants, on occasion the results may be satisfying. The present version of the "O Antiphons" is the result of literally years of experiment. As musicians know, each antiphon melody is slightly different, the Latin words

mas eve. This version may be so used. Since the Magnificat is fairly long, however, we felt that shorter scriptural texts might also be sung, relating to the different texts of the "O Antiphons," with the respective antiphon sung before and after. The melody given here is not strictly Gregorian Chant, but a more ancient psalm tone which A. Z. Idelsohn discovered among the isolated Jewish community of Yemen. By a happy coincidence, the tone is in the same mode as the "O Antiphons." It

being adjusted to a "melody-type"; this in turn is adjusted to the differing words. Since no one knows the original melody, I attempted with other musicians to recreate a probable archetype ("Urmelodie") and adapted singable words to this melody. After some years of experiment we came up with the texts offered here, which we find altogether singable.

The "O Antiphons" are, of course, designed to be used at Vespers before and after the Magnificat from December 17 to the day before Christ-

seems most appropriate to use this ancient Hebrew melody (which could have been known to Jesus, Mary and Joseph) together with the messianic antiphons leading to Christmas.

The "O Antiphons" have been described as a mosaic of the Old Testament. Their themes, as always in a Christian reading of the Bible, are broadly messianic, stressing the brightness of hope. Jesus is invoked under a series of titles, drawn largely from Isaiah, but in a sequence that must be intentional. They move historically from the beginning, before creation, to the very gates of Bethlehem. It seems more than coincidental, too, that the titles given to Jesus make an acrostic in Latin, which when read backwards means: "I will be tomorrow" ("Ero Cras")—an obvious (at least to the medieval mind) allusion to Christmas eve: *O Sapientia, Adonai, Radix, Clavis, Oriens, Rex, Emmanuel.*

The first antiphon is an apostrophe to Wisdom, the Logos, the Word of God. One is back at the beginning, in the recesses of eternity, Point Alpha, before the cosmos, reaching to Point Omega. Structurally, each antiphon resembles a traditional liturgical prayer: first, a worthy title; next, praise in terms of that title; finally, a petition relevant to that title. Wisdom encompasses and orders all things, strongly and sweetly. Our prayer is for the way of prudence. Wisdom must come and teach us. It is the insistent prayer of Advent: Come!

From eternity and creation we move to the manifestation of God's name, given in the fire of the burning bush and again with the Torah on Mount Sinai. The sacred name YHWH was long left unpronounced, replaced by the more generic title Adonai, meaning *my* Lord, not simply Lord. The Logos is here addressed in a more concrete, intimate way, as Lord and ruler of the chosen people. God gave the Torah as the way to life, to the first redemption, during the Exodus guided by Moses. Jesus himself will be our definitive Exodus, our final redemption. Again we ask him: Come!

Onward we move in sacred history, to Jesse's root. The Jesse tree is familiar in sacred art; one recalls the summit of stained glass in the Jesse window of Chartres Cathedral, and the humble Jesse trees found everywhere in the Middle Ages, fittingly now in a garden of New York's Cloisters museum. Jesse is David's father and an ancestor of Jesus. This antiphon is itself a mosaic of passages from Isaiah, especially chapters 11 and 52. As we move toward the first coming, our prayer becomes more urgent: Come and do not delay!

The expression "key of David" is suggested again by Isaiah in chapter 22, though it is the final book of the New Testament that applies the expression to Christ (3:7). As son of David, Jesus is heir and possessor of David's keys and scepter. After he rose from the dead he announced that all power was given him in heaven and on earth. It was this power that he communicated to Peter: "Whatever you bind on earth will be bound in heaven." Here the prayer "Come" is expanded and made more explicit, asking the Savior to free those who languish in the prison of sin. It was the primordial sin that fettered mankind, but these fetters are made tighter through personal transgression. Jesus will save us from both.

"O Oriens" is difficult to translate: dayspring, rising sun, dawn, orient.

Jesus is the radiance of his Father's splendor, the Sun of justice, the Light. Some of these titles occur in Zechariah (3:8 and 6:12). In the canticle of New Testament sung at Lauds, the Benedictus, we meet the phrase "Oriens ex alto." The venerable Zechariah asks that Jesus "enlighten those who sit in darkness and in the shadow of death." In the creed we profess our faith in him as "light of light." Malachi uses the phrase "sun of justice." This antiphon prays for enlightenment for all, both pagans and God's people. The sun god is one of the most familiar deities of cosmic religion, the sun naturally being associated with life, light and warmth. Mithraism, with its stress on sun worship, was a popular cult at the time of Christ. Its great feast day was December 25, and it is believed that this date was chosen as Christmas in reaction to this. At this time of the year the days begin to grow longer, the sun more visible. The first five antiphons, as Pius Parsch notes, "stemmed from a Jewish background." The Messiah was to be the fulfillment of Jewish expectations. Here, however, he is invoked as king of nations—the Gentiles—and the one desired by all. Both texts are suggested in the Old Testament: Jeremiah 10:7 and Haggai 2:8. Jesus will be the cornerstone binding both Jews and Gentiles into one. He would call himself by the same title in Matthew. Paul would later call him the peacemaker between Jew and Gentile (Ephesians 2:14 and Galatians 3:29). Man is fashioned from clay, the earth; Christ is true man, but has the special strength and binding power of rock.

The final "O Antiphon" suggests immediate fulfillment. Jesus is given his most intimate title—"God with us." All during Advent we have been singing the popular hymn "O come, O come, Emmanuel." The term, once again, is from Isaiah. In chapter 7 we read the familiar text: "A virgin will conceive and bear a son, and his name shall be called Emmanuel." Here we call on him not by some exalted title, but by what has almost become his nickname, But we quickly recall that he, though one of us, is still king and lawgiver, the expected of nations and their Savior. Again we hear allusions to Isaiah who (32:22) calls the Lord judge, lawgiver, king, who will save us. The phrase "expected of nations" takes us back to Gene-

sis and Jacob's dying prophecy: "The scepter will not pass from Judah, nor a ruler from his thigh, till he comes that is to be sent. He is the expectation of the nations." This final antiphon ends, unlike the others, with a second apostrophe, this time most explicit of all: "O Lord our God."

The "O Emmanuel" happens to be my favorite of the seven antiphons. One reason may be the cluster of titles—almost a microcosm of the messianic prophecies. Another is surely the sense of climax arising from the sequence of O's. Experience has shown that this reaction is not only personal. When the "O Antiphons" are sung—either at Mass or during some prayer or Scripture service—day after day before Christmas eve, a truly Adventan feeling of anticipation builds up. I have also found it effective as a signature song during a series on public broadcasting called "Sacred Music of the West." It seemed a joyous summary of revelation from Alpha to Omega, from creation to the eschaton, as well as a celebration of both Advents.

THE O ANTIPHONS FOR ADVENT
With PSALM VERSE and Magnificat

Adapted—with English Words
C.J. McNASPY S.J.

1. O___ Ho - ly_ Wis - dom Who came forth from the Mouth of the Most High, Who re
2. O___ Might-y Lord Our_ God! and Ruler of the House of Is - ra - el, Who di
3. O___ Root_ of_ Jes - se! Who are a Sign for the Na - tions, be - for
4. O___ Key_ of_ Da - vid! and Scepter of the House of Is - ra - el, Who o
5. O___ Light_ from the_ East! and Splendor of Light e - ter - nal, Who are
6. O___ King_ of_ Na - tions! for Whom the Na - tions_ have longed, Who are
7. O___ E - man - u - el! Who are our King and Ru - ler, Who are

1. from end to end of all cre-a - - tion, mightily and sweet-ly or - der-in
2. appear in the burning bush to Mos - es Your_ proph - et, and on Mt. Sin-ai did give him_ Yo
3. Whom the voices of Kings are closed in still - - ness, to Whom the gen-tiles lift_ up
4. pen and there is none_ who_ clo - ses, Who close and no one o -
5. the Sun of jus - tice ev - er - last - ing, Come and let Your light_
6. the cornerstone to join_ all_ na - tions, Who bring all_ men_ to
7. the Expectation of the na - - - tions, the Sal - va - tion of all_

1. all things O_ come, to show_ us Your_ peo - ple, the_ paths_ of wis - dor
2. Law, O_ come, and give_ us Your_ might-y arm, in Your pow-er re - deem_ us.
3. their prayer O_ come, and de - liv - er Your_ peo - ple, has - ten Lord_ and save_ us.
4. - pens. O_ come, and free_ us from_ pri - son, from_ death_ and dark - nee
5. shine forth, O_ come, and let_ Your light_ shine on us, in_ death_ and dark - nee
6. geth-er, O_ come, and res - cue all_ man - kind, that from dust You cre - a - ted
7. man-kind, O_ come, and bring_ us sal - va - tion, O_ Lord_ Al - might - y.

PSALM VERSES

Ancient Hebrew Cl

1. { Sing with joy O daughter of Si - on, be filled with gladness O Je - ru - sa - lem
   { For be - hold the Lord is com - ing, and He will renew Je - - ru - sa - lem

2. { Now the Lord will come our Pro - tec - tor, the Holy One of Is - ra - el.
   { And the Lord will wear a king-ly crown, and He will rule from sea to sea.

3. { For the Lord will bring jus - tice, and peace will reign a - bun - dant-ly.
   { All the kings of earth will a - dore Him, all nations shall serve Him

4. { Come O Lord and show Your coun-te - nance, and we shall be com - fort - ed.
   { And in that day will shine a great light, for He will conquer the dark - ness

5. { For His going forth is like the light of dawn, to bring the ever - - last - ing day.
   { And when we His people shall see His face, our hearts will be filled with joy.

6. { Praise the Lord all you na - tions, pro - claim His glory all you peo - ple.
   { For His Name is praised in all the world, and His peace will be with all man-kind

7. { For a Virgin shall conceive and bring forth a Son, and His Name shall be called E - man - u - el.
   { And He shall be called the Might-y God, and His rule will be for - - ev - er.

KEEPING CHRISTMAS

Family Ritual for Celebrating

Gabe Huck

Forty-five minutes is a long Christmas in many homes. Though it is true that the main point of a pilgrimage is the journeying, not the goal, nothing that brief could justify the risks and adventures of a good Advent. That's a weak analogy, perhaps, for Christmas is not so much the destination of Advent as it is a second movement to Advent's first. The two surround the winter solstice. On the one side we hear—hearts and scriptures echoing one another—of the fear in being human (it is dark in

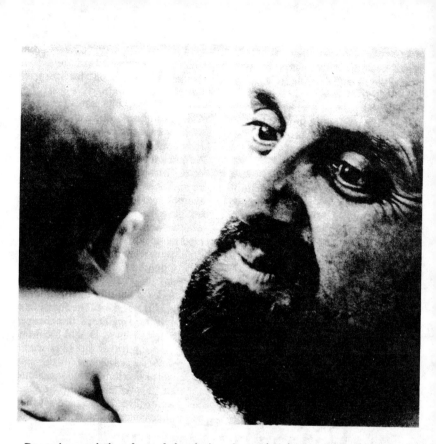

December and that fear of the dark roots all the others), of waiting and how fine it can be, of promises whispered and spoken and shouted across centuries and across breakfast tables.

Gabe Huck does parish work in liturgy and education in Brighton, Colorado. He is the editor of a quarterly packet published by The Liturgical Conference. The publication is called *Major Feasts and Seasons*; the first issue, a total parish approach to Advent, is available now from: The Liturgical Conference, 1330 Massachusetts Avenue N.W., Washington, D.C. 20005.

A good Advent makes the fear, the waiting and the promises dance and play through the community's life in the four weeks before Christmas.

But what of the other side of the solstice, when one wait ends, one promise is fulfilled, one fear is made a hope: the sun halts in its retreat from these northern lands and begins giving a minute or two more of light each day? Christians were not the first to place the birthday of their founder on the birthday of the sun.

Nor were we the first to say such a birthday should be marked with joyful celebration and extended over a period of many days. Probably our only distinction is the sad one of proving that the energy put into preparation (energy here embracing time and money as it normally does) has absolutely no relation to the depth, length or joy of the festival. How has it ever happened that *Christmas* can be over and gone, totally wiped out, by the morning of December 26? Or even by the morning of December 25?

My purpose is not to attack what "they" have done to Christmas. I would rather wonder what we might do with it or let it do for us. Christmas, like the more ancient winter holidays it absorbed, is a crucial moment in the rhythm of life. By one means or another, such festivals catch drooping, even despairing human spirits, invite them to sing and to dance and to hear the human story and to take comfort if not exultation. Such a festival is a work of art in time. The good ritual sense and artistry of believers in Jesus of many places and centuries filled this high winter moment in the rhythm of human life with a multitude of good ways not only to hear and affirm our identity as Christians, but to be caught up in experiences of it.

Like a good snowperson, then, a good festival is folk art. It is created not by research and rubric, but by need and imagination. There are signs that we may be a part of a renewal of the art. Households (a bet-ter word than families because it is broader) are discovering and redis-covering what makes for a human festival. Those who are interested have opportunities now not only to try on their own, but to communicate about their efforts. (The success of *The Alternate Christmas Catalogue* in its first and second editions shows how many folks won't give up on Christmas. If you want a copy this year, write to Alternatives, 1500 Farragut Street N.W., Washington D.C. 20011.)

Our starting point is that Christmas is a season, not just a day. Whether by observing the 12 days (or possibly fewer if, with the present church calendar, we keep Epiphany always on a Sunday), or the whole time to Candlemas on February 2, the rites call for a savoring. Within that season, all the regular parts of life together (meals, prayers, activities shared) can be made at least a little bit different: something of the season gets into each of them.

Beyond this, we look for what is once-a-year about these days. It is important to share in the decisions of what the household will do, and it is important that we stick with what goes well. Year after year it will be the repetition that becomes Christmas for us. Doing the household's rites of Christmas over and over will give to children and to adults too a sense of security, of belonging, as well as an identity. What these customs will be is partly a manner of reflecting on what has been good and what has been destructive of the

43

spirit in past seasons. That is a beginning. It may hold surprises. Listen carefully, for the seeds of your Christmas keeping may be in the simplest of yearly rituals.

Remember that the function of ritual (and that's used very broadly here to take in any of the annual household habits for the season) is to take us beyond words to a realm where our whole selves can be expressive. In the ritual we give expression in symbol to our feelings and convictions; the good ritual in turn strengthens such feelings and convictions. The principle is the same whether we think of making the sign of the cross, standing for the national anthem, or kissing a child good night. But ritual is as demanding as it is necessary and powerful. Without care, ritual can become empty, fraudulent, destructive. It would not be difficult to name national Christmastime rituals that are such. If the ideas discussed below would be out of place in your household, perhaps they can serve as starting points for what would be expressive of your life and your faith about Christmas. Beginnings can be awkward and self-conscious, for we are not a people at ease with the idea of playing or praying. But play and pray, celebrate, keep the feast; we must if the faltering feelings we have for the world-shaking potential of a Christmas kept well are to survive.

Making Christmas a season depends on what we have done with Advent, and on what we do with the day itself. Examining household practices and the parish rituals for Christmas eve and day are a beginning. Especially if children are involved, the timing of the community Eucharist for Christmas is important lest it be only a "time out" from what appears to be the "real" Christmas: the gifts. One answer may be a very special Eucharist for families with younger children (when well done, it will attract all ages) just after supper on Christmas eve. If Advent has been doing its work, and if large numbers are involved in planning, setting up, and singing, and if every person is encouraged to bring something like a bell or a candle, then this liturgy can be a very real part of Christmas for adults and children. A special kind of family Christmas eve meal can, over the years, become an integral part of beginning the season. Another time for such a parish liturgy (and again the liturgy itself must be planned and done well) is about mid-day on Christmas, between the gifts and the feast, when the rhythm of the day allows the leisure for playfulness and prayerfulness.

The Christmas tree is one of the great pre-Christian rituals of the winter festival. In the season of death and cold and blacks and whites there is this green and almost warm thing to comfort and give hope. But we have questions today about slaughtering trees in the millions. Some, often for other reasons, turn to artificial trees. Some construct their "tree" of wood or papier-maché or tinkertoys. Some decide to at least search out and cut their own tree. Some decorate a living tree outside. Some buy a small living tree to be kept indoors a few days, then taken outside and planted when the ground thaws. The matter is important, for our symbols should express our convictions. Just as important is how we give the tree a place in our homes: how we make room for it, how we decorate it, how we gather around it, how individually we make certain to have the time to reflect and ponder on it. Just as the family together decides on the tree, so together all can decide on ways to gather around it.

The tree can be the central symbol of the season, but not if it is ten days or two weeks old when Christmas arrives. Advent has its own visual elements, and they lead into Christmas. There will be no way to prolong Christmas, to make it the season it needs to be, if its symbols are exhausted, powerless, by December 25. A good Advent fills the days before Christmas: there is no void into which an early tree must be stuffed. Let it come just a day or two before Christmas at a time when some fine hours can be spent in clothing it.

The tree decorations can be one of those fine rituals that bind the years together. In our own family, we have come quite naturally to add a few things every year, so that our tree gathers up all our Christmas times together: large balls of cotton from years in Oklahoma, many kinds of pine cones and nuts gathered at Christmas during east coast years, shapes of once brightly painted papier-maché, year-old cookies, wooden shapes, popcorn and cranberries. Some we have made, many were

gifts. It takes hours to do the tree because each is so precious. Some the children can share, some they can be told about. There is no room on the tree for anything less dear to us.

The putting up and the taking down of the tree should mark two major moments in the Christmas season. Epiphany may be the ideal day for taking it down and concluding the season with a party. What is done with the tree afterward gets some thought; putting it out for trash is a sign too.

Along with decorating the tree, the whole house may be made festive. Here especially it is a growth of the Advent mood and its visual elements. As with the tree clothing, there can be additions from year to year as our symbols tell us very beautifully who we have been and so something of who we are, this household. And that kind of identifying, of making community, carries on the deepest function of human festivity.

The crèche is another important visual sign of the season. The figures and setting can be made of the cheapest material, but they should be beautiful. In so much of our lives we are practically forced to opt for the ugly, usually for economic reasons. Better here to pay to have someone carve just two or three figures and set them amid pine cones or straw, or to make them carefully of play dough and paint them, or to paint them on the sides of small boxes. Again, each year can see the addition of a figure.

One child might be given the special task on Christmas eve of setting up the nativity figures. Perhaps the family likes to make candles and some of the most beautiful ones can be placed within this scene. Then when the family can gather for some minutes without pressure, on the eve or the morning, the candles are lighted, the Christmas story is told or read, and the figure of the baby is put in place as a Christmas song is sung. Then, as may have been the custom during Advent or with keeping Chanukah, there are some moments of silence in the candlelight.

Sometimes there is a custom of blessing the tree or the crèche. Here especially a group may be creative. They might decide to gather around the tree, join hands and dance around it singing its traditional praise: "O Christmas Tree." There can be a blessing too with water that has itself been blessed.

"The legend of Christmas gifts suggests they were originally rare things, tokens of love and respect. Something precious is sacrificed when these qualities are forgotten" (Betty Nickerson, *Celebrate the Sun,* p. 114,

Lippincott, 1969). "I wish you had said, 'Ann, for a present this Christmas I will teach you the names of all the constellations and the names of all the stars in them'" (Jessamyn West in *Redbook,* December 1971). "Jung insisted that 'the creative activity of imagination frees man from his bondage to the "nothing but" and raises him to the status of one who plays.' What right have we to take this rich capital of a child's playfulness and spend it recklessly on spiritless toys from a factory? . . . Limiting the number of Christmas gifts—even to one toy from both parents—is telling the child not only that he can't have everything but also that you can't give everything. . . . In the end, there is only one gift to our children, to be given at Christmas, Chanukah, on the way to Mecca, or whenever: the treasures of our time and talk, exactly what children want the most" (Colman McCarthy in *The Washington Post,* December 2, 1973).

There you have kernels from the three pieces that help me most to think about the giving of gifts at Christmas. Part of developing a sense of "season," of a spirit or a mood that pervades the days at this time of year, is grasping the totality of things like gift-giving. That doesn't mean that everyone can make gifts, but it does mean that the whole process of planning, selecting or making, and the giving itself is important. Our Christmas is to embody a notion of creation that is filled with ethical and ecological implications. It is in the ritual of gifts that these are incarnate. It is especially helpful to think of the many gifts we have to give that share self rather than a thing—like teaching the names of the stars, like time and talk. These kinds of gifts can be prolonged during the whole season of Christmas, can extend the festivity, can give a uniqueness to each of the twelve days. It is, in typical families, a challenge to make the receiving of gifts only one element among many in the keeping of Christmas. That is not only a challenge to do exciting things with the other aspects of the day and season, it is an opportunity to delve into what gifts can be when you let imagination play with the idea. And it is an exercise in timing, for good gifts should be savored—another reason for a Christmas of at least twelve days.

The Christmas meal is itself a gift. Its preparation, another rite that moves us from Advent to Chrismas, can involve every member of the household. There are almost always some traditions about what is served, and as children grow they can acquire their own specialty to be added to the menu. The time of the meal can be set so that there is no competition: the graciousness and leisure can be a model for meals together during the ordinary times. A very special blessing of that meal can be the responsibility of some one member of the household and might involve simple song, movement, toasts and spoken prayers of thanks. Singing "Happy Birthday" to the Lord Jesus may be just right at some point; at least it's a song everyone will sing.

As more and more people live further from their extended families, the Christmas dinner may become an occasion for strengthening the ties in the newer form of extended families. Two or more households (and a household may be just one person) join together for this meal. Few occasions will do more to create strong ties between friends and between children and adults other than their parents.

Food is also one of the ways the season is created, for there can be different sorts of customs for several of the twelve days. Or it could become the custom that the St. Stephen's day dinner is planned and prepared by the father, the St. John's day dinner is prepared by the oldest child, and the Holy Family Sunday dinner is a meal out. Again, if it seems to make folks happy, remember it and do it next year.

Christmas cards are normally an Advent activity, and in many homes this is the best way to handle it, but any activity so tied to the Christmas season and so consuming of time and money ought to be consciously planned. Why do we do it? is the first question. Then how. And is it for the whole family, and so an area where the task should be divided, or does each member have a list of friends? And what is the card to be? Each year there are more well done cards available, but many would find it cheaper to check with a local printer and see what the cost would be to run off a one-color reproduction of a simple drawing by one member of the family in a quantity sufficient to send to the whole Christmas card list. Printed on one side of a heavy stock, the 8½x11 sheet can be folded twice, closed with a small piece of tape, and be its own mailer. And two-thirds of the area on one side is free for writing notes. It's almost bound to be less expensive than buying cards and is much more personnel; creating the card becomes part of keeping the season.

But give some thought to waiting for the Christmas season itself to write your notes and do the mailing. Then you not only make it more leisurely, but it becomes a part of extending Christmas for you and for the ones receiving the cards.

The second day of Christmas is the feast of Stephen and might be a day of testimony about Jesus. Go caroling and sing the Christmas proclamation. ("What are you, nuts or something, don't you know Christmas is over?") Song in a household can begin to be natural at Christmas when there are more songs around that we aren't afraid to try together. Buy kazoos for those who just can't carry the tunes anyway. And listen for some of the unusual carols and songs that will have a special force because we haven't heard them so many times.

The third day of Christmas is the feast of John the apostle. A happy tradition has this as a day for blessing the wine, perhaps because of a legend that John drank poisoned wine and was not harmed. Set the bottles of wine on the table and join in blessing them with extended hands, perhaps using the Jewish blessing: "Blessed art thou, O Lord our God, ruler of the universe, for you have given us the fruit of the vine." And then a toast to the beloved disciple.

The fourth and fifth days of Christmas, December 28 and 29, are of a different kind. The first is the feast of the holy innocents, the children of Bethlehem said to have been killed by Herod in an effort to be rid of Jesus. It seems strange that this particular memory should be placed before us— but only until we think for a moment on what happened on December 29, 1890 at Wounded Knee in South Dakota. There was a massacre that day also, children and helpless adults slaughtered by United States soldiers. So the 29th too is a feast of holy innocents. Both say something for how the very preciousness of human life which we celebrate in this season needs to be guarded from the violence of society and of self. Since Christmas of 1972 the whole season must be, especially for people of the United States, marked with the memory of the senseless and cruel bombing of North Vietnam by President Nixon.

That is the kind of a world Jesus was born to, and we also. These days might be, within a time of feasting, a moment to fast and to lament and to confront, at whatever level we can, our own complicity in the way innocents continue to die by starvation and by war. There is a poem by Kenneth Patchen which ends:

They are blowing out the candles, Mary. . . .
The world is a thing gone mad tonight.
O hold Him tenderly, dear Mother,
For His is a Kingdom in the hearts of men.

The story of the innocents of Bethlehem is found in Matthew's Gospel. One account of the innocents of Wounded Knee is found in *Black Elk Speaks* by John Neihardt.

The Sunday between Christmas and New Year's is celebrated as the feast of the Holy Family. Perhaps the regular feature of this day ought to be doing something irregular, spur-of-the-moment plans for the kind of thing a family just never does together. For some that might be taking a walk. For others, going to a sports event. For others, going to a museum. For others, a snowball fight —or challenging the family across the street to a snowball fight.

Some years ago *McCall's* carried an article by Barbara Rohde about her search for New Year's Eve. Leaving the old and welcoming the new, she says, has historically prompted humanity's greatest ritual-making. Till now. We need it no less, but we somehow manage to let the moment slip by. Within the household, the eve might be given to games (fortune-telling is a tradition of the night), to drawing or writing the highs and lows of the dying year, to taking everyone's weight and height and hopes for the year ahead—to be carefully preserved and read on next New

Year's Eve. And to some rather wild noisemaking at the midnight bell—outside, of course.

New Year's Day itself (by a tradition longer than football games will ever have) is the day for visiting friends. Emerson wrote that friendship "should be surrounded with ceremonies and respects and not crushed into corners." This is a day for these ceremonies of friendship. Families seldom visit families anymore, and that's a great loss. On all the warm weather holidays we run in our separate directions. New Year's deserves better.

If all twelve days of Christmas have been special with songs, gifts, meals, candles, adventures and stories (it would be wonderful to have a book that the family would reread together each year during these days, perhaps a collection of fairy tales, or C. S. Lewis' Narnia stories), you will be ready to conclude with Epiphany. The party could come before or after the things of Christmas have been put away. Christmas music and lots of incense set the mood for the meal. Friends might be invited to the meal or at least for dessert.

Dessert carries with it a fine Epiphany custom. A wonderful cake is baked—with three almonds hidden in it. The persons who get almonds in their cake become the three magi. They are then solemnly dressed in the grandest bathrobes and drapes and pieces of material available. Perhaps one of the children will have made crowns for them. A procession forms around the magi. Someone carries chalk, someone has the blessed water, someone the branch for sprinkling, someone the incense. Another may carry a cross and others may carry candles.

Singing "We Three Kings" or whatever everyone knows, the procession goes from one room of the house to another. In each room, everyone stops while one person asks a blessing on that room: "May my bedroom be blessed with warmth and good dreams" or "May our kitchen be blessed with sharing in food and in work, with good smells and pleasant talk." Then the blessed water is sprinkled around and, at least by the front door, the traditional marking is done above the door:

19+C+M+B+76, for the year and the three magi (Caspar, Melchior and Balthasar). A final prayer might be the one taken from the Liturgy of the Hours: "Visit this home, we ask you, God. Chase away from it anything that might harm us. Send your angels to live here with us. May your blessings be always upon us." Then the three magi preside over games and partying.

In the rhythm of our year, the rest of January is rather quiet, a rest before the preparation for and work of Lent begins. There are a few days that could be celebrated: January 15, the birthday of Martin Luther King, Jr.; January 17, the feast of Saint Anthony, patron of all the animals that live with people; and finally February 2, a concluding feast of lights when all candles can be gathered and blessed and the stories of Anna and Simeon heard.

We are in need of the good signs, the rituals and the customs, that express beyond words who we are. Seasons like Christmas offer the high moments when our basic communities focus on some of what we believe living and living together is all about.

We are not beyond rejoicing in the sun's birthday, believing the world to be a most special place, and making small epiphanies that signify and realize the divine in the midst of human community.

AN UNTIDY SEASON

Ralph A. Keifer

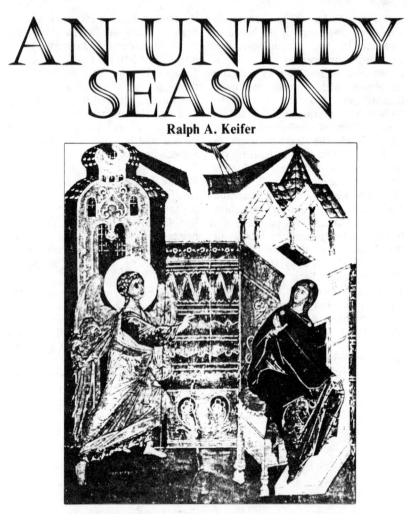

Advent isn't exactly a comfortable season. And I don't mean just the ice on the windshield and the certain prospect of January bills. Advent's liturgy has a strangeness about it that won't be tamed by caroling that begins at Thanksgiving or the cuddly prospect of the sweet baby in the manger. The measured sobriety of the Advent Masses clashes with the festive rush of streets and stores. And the urgency of the readings clashes with what we generally chose to call religion. The Advent Gospels begin with the thunder of the last judgment —hardly something that we care to make a matter of daily meditation. And if the thought of judgment is vaguely discomforting, it's also not very real to us. Chances are the second coming isn't going to happen tomorrow morning, next week, or next year. The threat of dread cosmic judgment grips us no more than the "eager longing" of Advent hymns. We may be momentarily bemused by such thoughts, but we are neither excited nor awed by them. The wild hairy figure of John the Baptist dominates the next two Sundays. He is even less help. Folks who go around in funny costumes telling us that we ought to repent because the reign of God is at hand don't have much to do with comfortable Catholicity. In our hearts, we know that old J.B. would have been as much embarrassment to the parish as the fleas which were sure to have inhabited his coat of camel's hair. The fourth Sunday, possibly, has a more familiar note. Then it is Mary who comes to the fore in the Gospel. But Father squirms at the lectern, assuring us that Mary is still important—though the vigil lights have gone out and the statue was taken away with the last remodeling. All in all, none of this seems to make for a lot of instant relevance.

Just how are we supposed to identify with this strange season? Its purple

Ralph A. Keifer, professor of liturgy at St. Mary's Seminary and University in Baltimore, is an associate editor for *Worship* magazine, and has published articles in *Worship*, *Commonweal*, and other national periodicals.

sobriety contrasts with the tinsel festival of an American Christmas that begins with October advertising. And for all the expectancy that we feel for the coming of Christmas, the coming of Christ seems remote, even unlikely. We can, of course, feel guilty. We can feel guilty that Christians no longer thrill to the prospect of Christ's coming in glory, guilty that we are no longer overawed by the threat of judgment. Even the peculiar figure of that prophet on the edge of the desert can arouse us to a twinge of nostalgia for a more rough and ready religion. And if we are no longer moved by the maid of Nazareth in the same way that our ancestors were, perhaps we should look back to pieties we no longer practice with a sense of lost innocence. Should we, perhaps, share the Gospels' sense of immediacy? Is the Advent preacher right when he tells us that there is something wrong with *us* because we can't quite make the spirit of the Advent season our own? But the problem is that guilt isn't the keynote of the season either. Feeling guilty is a long way from the sense of joy that is so pervasive in the Advent liturgy. Joy is so characteristic of the season that virtually every responsorial psalm is a psalm of rejoicing. *Rejoice,* the prophet says. *Rejoice,* says St. Paul. They don't say: "Feel guilty because you aren't rejoicing." They just say: *Rejoice.*

But it's not exactly the rejoicing of the office party either. The liturgy says *Rejoice* as it is decked in sober purple, and its says it into the teeth of the night of winter (at least in the

Western Hemisphere, where the season originated). Such odd churchly behavior ought to give us pause. Why not something brighter than purple if we are supposed to be rejoicing? Or why not take up the dread judgment bit, and skip the rejoicing stuff? And if we were to take the Baptist seriously, would we really want to *rejoice*? Locusts and wild honey and camel's hair aren't exactly what we have in mind when we wish people "season's greetings." If we can't have instant relevance, how about at least a little consistency?

For it seems to be such an untidy season. Here a comforting passage, there a threat; crazy John at the edge of the desert and meek Mary at Nazareth; the purple of mourning and the songs of rejoicing. The Last Day (on the first Sunday) is a day of wrath, and we pray to greet it with joy. What a mess! No instant relevance, and not even a tidy thematic.

How, then, should we deal with Advent? As a tidy heirloom, perhaps, annually dusted off for a churchly *For Auld Lang Syne*? After all, sensitive people don't throw out antiques just because they can't be used in the kitchen or at the dining room table. They keep them, with a respect for the past and a nostalgia for (supposedly) simpler and less troubled times. Maybe we should dutifully celebrate the Advent liturgy in remembrance of our beloved ancestors in the faith. Or maybe we can go modern and simplify it into a tidier thematic. The passages from Isaiah on justice have a contemporary ring,

don't they? Couldn't we just skip that awful first Sunday with its threat of last judgment?

I suppose we could do one of those things—and some conventional preaching and hymnody attempt to do just that—either to create a "let's pretend" liturgy or to ignore the very abrasive edges of the season. But there is another possibility, and that is to attempt to penetrate what the Bible and the liturgy say during this season—without asking them to say what we would like them to say, and without asking them to say it in a way we would like to hear it. To do that, we have to rid ourselves of the

notion that either the Bible or the liturgy pursues a tidy thematic. Most of the time, they don't. Both Bible and liturgy are concerned with the relationship between God and his people. And relationships, in case anybody

54

And while the passages we read in the liturgy are inevitably grounded in the past, they are there to reflect something of the meaning of *today, now.*

With this in mind, it is possible to begin to get something of a handle on the peculiar season of Advent. By and large, we don't get very big doses of information. After all, we already know that the ministry of John the Baptist preceded that of Jesus, and that Mary was the mother of Jesus. Nothing terribly new, and nothing terribly informative. Advent's thematic, if it can be called such, is so simple that it's not apt to make the banners this year—God is present to us.

Now there's something with perennial possibilities, even to people who don't warm up much to the prospect of the second coming. And Advent looks to that great feast of God's presence to us—Christmas. The Advent season's concern is to linger over the fact of his presence, to ponder something of the depth of its meaning. For God's presence, in biblical terms, is less an idea than a stubbornly concrete fact of life—so concrete that God's presence to his world is through his Son, who became one of us. And who became one of us to unite us to the Father.

hasn't noticed, aren't especially tidy —even when they don't approach the breadth and depth of the relationship between God and his people. We also have to get rid of the notion that Bible and liturgy are necessarily communicating *information* about the relationship between God and his people. In many cases, biblical passages, especially biblical passages in the liturgy, are concerned with the *meaning* of the relationship between God and his people, not with new information.

We can, of course, approach this as another ho-hum sublime religious teaching about something that happened long ago and far away. After all, it has been nearly two thousand years since the incarnation. But what the liturgy, with its biblical readings, is trying to say is that the whole matter isn't ho-hum and it isn't past; it's happening now. God continues to identify with us. Christ continues to be present.

One of the things that continually throws us in our understanding of the liturgical year is that we generally miss the meaning of another great feast—the ascension. It may seem odd to bring this up in a discussion of Advent, but I think it's necessary if we are to make any sense at all of Advent. We tend to read all the mysteries of the Christian year as though they were merely past events—mainly because we've got it in our heads that Christ's ascension was a kind of farewell to this world. If Christ has "gone back to heaven" then we have to read all the other great feasts as though they referred merely to time past, to events that happened a long time ago. Or, alternatively, we can look to an indefinite future (so indefinite that Christ himself said that only the Father knows the day and the hour) when Christ will "come back again." Either way, we have to resort to pious tricks to identify with the liturgy and its biblical readings—"wait for the birth of Jesus" (when we knows it has already happened), or "look forward to the second coming" (which really doesn't grip us).

The fact of the matter is that the ascension is *not* Christ's farewell to our world. It is the end of his *visible* presence to his disciples, and the beginning of what, for want of better words, might be described as his larger presence to the world. The as-

cended Christ is no longer bound to the confines of time (the reign of Tiberias Caesar) or space (Jerusalem and Galilee), but in his Spirit is present to all of us. The New Testament never speaks of a *second* coming, but only of Christ's coming (i.e., of a persistent active presence already in motion) and of his *appearance* (parousia), that is, of the day when his presence will be wonderfully manifest. Any "looking forward" that we do is grounded in what is *already happening*. And we don't have to become "contemporaries of Jesus." The Son of God became one of us to be our contemporary here and now.

One of the most appealing features of the Advent season is that it doesn't allow this great fact to be swaddled in sentimentality or rationalized into abstraction. The doom and gloom of the First Sunday of Advent's Gospel may jar us, but it has the distinct advantage of suggesting that the God who is present to use isn't exactly a warm fuzzy. He's downright spooky and spine-chilling—not, most likely, what most of us would like him to be. This is a God who will not be tamed, either by cute Christmas cards or even by our polite liturgy. He eludes our rationalizations and he escapes our comprehension. He's not what we think he is. In many ways, this goes against the human grain. It would be so much nicer, after all, to have a more reasonable God who can be tidily defined, categorized, pigeonholed. But that's not the God of the Bible and the liturgy.

Oddly enough, it is the very strangeness of that First Sunday that can strike a contemporary chord, especially for Catholics at the present time. One of the features of recent American Catholic experience is the shattering of old certitudes and the disappearance of familiar religious landmarks. There is a wistfulness for the time when we "had it all together." The jarring note of the First Sunday of Advent suggests that we don't even *need* to have it all together. The God who calls us is not always found in the familiar, the stable, and the comfortable. The security of faith does not rest in owning a comfortably familiar set of beliefs and practices, but in being called by a God who persists in a refusal to be governed by our own petty presuppositions.

And if we now belong to a less-than-

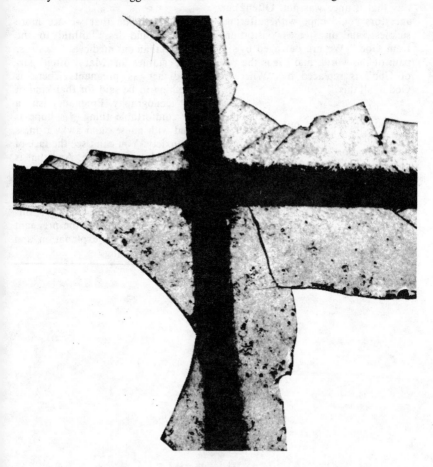

triumphant Church, we also live in a less than confident world. There is something paradoxical in celebrating a festival of God's presence in a world in which the absence of God is so vividly felt. We are troubled by things which never troubled our ancestors with such intensity. Faith is something that can no longer be taken for granted. And evil in the world is felt as a threat to faith in a way that it once was not. Often, our ancestors could cope with suffering, sickness, and disaster as "visitations from God." We are outraged by the pain of the world, and "It is the will of God" is replaced by "Where is God in all this?"

Advent approaches our question—not with an "explanation," but with an affirmation: God's presence often comes under the cover of darkness and defeat. We are met with a paradox—God is often most present when he seems most distant. The very mood and color of the liturgy grapple with this paradox—songs of rejoicing in garments of mourning, looking to the light in the darkness of winter. It is a dominant strain in the biblical readings. The Old Testament prophecies of hope and deliverance which are the heart of the season did not come at Israel's hour of triumph. They were wrung out of defeat and exile. The Baptist comes from the desolation of the desert to proclaim the way of the Lord. And the Lord of the earth is born in poverty and obscurity in a backwater province.

It is unfortunate that we are more inhibited (and less faithful to the Gospels) than our medieval ancestors, whose statues of Mary often portrayed her as pregnant. There is something to be said for that kind of blunt iconography. Pregnancy isn't a very comfortable thing. Its hope is tinged with nausea and awkwardness and anxiety. You can't see the face of the one who is to come. And that is what Advent is about. The splendor of God's presence is hidden in the fragmentary untidiness of our lives, and lies beneath the pain of this world. The season, like the pregnant Virgin, is short on explanation and heavy with meaning.

Advent Projects for Children

Janaan Manternach

A couple of years ago I was visiting some friends during Advent. Hanging from the light over the dining room table was a strange looking box. On the box were little doors that were to be opened each day during the season. Several of them were standing open so I peeked in. Words met my eyes—words that spoke of how God comes. "God comes to us in life."

"God comes to us in music." "God comes to us in people." "God comes to us in a new day." A feeling of genuine delight stole over me. As I was marveling over the box with its messages, Thomas, at three years the oldest of the two children in the family, began talking to me about the box and breakfast time and Poppa reading from the Bible and Momma telling them about Aavent. Before Thomas was finished, Neil, aged two, interrupted to tell me that this was their Advent Box.

Janaan Manternach, O.S.F., is co-author of *Life, Love, Joy* religious education series.

In early April the following year I was babysitting with these children while their parents were visiting friends in New York City. I had given Thomas his bath and we were on our way downstairs for breakfast, hand-in-hand. About the seventh step down Thomas paused to ask me if I knew how God comes to us. It was too early in the morning to venture a proper answer, so I just looked at him in a bemused way. He sensed that I might not know, so he lovingly answered his own question mostly to himself, but also with me in mind as we continued walking down the stairs. "God comes to us in people. Janaan, you're a people!" "God comes to us in a new day. This is a new day, isn't it?"

Tears welled up in my eyes as I spontaneously picked Thomas up and hugged him until he wiggled to get down.

I had forgotten about the Advent Box and the messages it contained, but Thomas had not. It had become a part of his memory, imagination, and experience because he had celebrated the meaning of Advent in a simple, concrete way with his family. They made a daily ritual out of the coming of God into their lives as a way to live out the season of Advent.

WHAT IS ADVENT?

Their family preparation for Christmas during Advent made a lot of sense to me. Christmas is the celebration of LIFE in life. Teilhard de Chardin spoke of the world as the "divine milieu." All of life is graced by the presence of Jesus Christ. His entry into it makes a difference in the quality that life has for each person no matter who, what or where he/she is. This is my belief. Therefore, Christmas is, for me, a celebration of the coming of Christ into the world. Christmas is the celebration of the mystery of the incarnation, of God with us.

Advent, then, is an initiation into the mystery of the incarnation. It is a time of prayerful preoccupation with God's presence in life through his Son Jesus. It is also a time of recalling why Jesus comes into the world: to overcome evil, to add new meaning to life, to show us a better way to live, to fill our emptiness, to provide an answer to the ultimate question: "What is life all about?"

Advent, as Thomas and Neil's box suggests, is a time to remember that God is with us in the ordinary happenings that make up each of our days. He is with us in good times and bad. He cares and he makes a big difference in our search for meaning in the face of life's ambiguities.

A season like Advent provides us with an occasion to become more and more open to what our belief in Jesus is, particularly as it affirms and accepts fully Jesus' promise: "I came that they might have life and have it to the full" (Jn. 10:10). He has come, yet he is continually coming to us in our daily experience. Advent openness to his coming is urged in the

Book of Revelation: "Here I stand, knocking at the door," says Jesus. "If anyone hears me calling and opens the door, I will enter his house and have supper with him, and he with me" (Rev. 3:20).

This openness and expectancy blend well with the expectancy in the air during the days that precede Christmas. People bustle around shopping for and wrapping gifts, baking, decorating, sending cards, and greeting strangers as well as acquaintances. A feeling of urgency fills the air. This aspect of our culture—in spite of its frequent overcommercialization—can remind us that we have been touched by the mystery of the incarnation, that the presence of Jesus with us is a cause for a fuller and deeper sense of what his coming into our lives is all about.

The expectancy and openness that is expressed in our celebration of Advent echoes centuries of longing for a Messiah. People like Isaiah, John the Baptist, and most of all, Mary exemplify this as the true meaning of Advent. A rich resource that we have for cultivating this attitude within ourselves and within our children is the Advent liturgy, particularly the daily Scripture readings. The liturgy can enrich and give meaning to the expectancy for Christ's coming that we are experiencing. Our experience, in turn, can help us identify with millions of Christians and Jews who waited and struggled over thirty centuries to open their hearts to God's coming.

HOW CELEBRATE ADVENT?

Any teaching about Advent, then, needs to encourage an openness and sensitivity to what is happening in our lives right now, remembering that Jesus comes into our lives each day. We need to recognize Jesus in the care and concern of a friend, in the listening ear and in the helping hand. We need to recognize Jesus in ourselves in a way that compels us to minister to and to serve others. Advent is a time of loving presence, both on his part and on ours. The Lord *is* visiting his people. And he is visiting his people in and through our daily lives.

I, therefore, see Advent as a special opportunity to guide children into a greater openness to life as a sign of God's presence. It is a time to foster in them the natural wonder they have when they see a flower, a burning candle, a bird, a skyscraper, a bug, a baby, an old man and woman. It is a time to tell them that God is with them in all that surrounds them.

Advent could be the great symphonic moment in a year's time as we celebrate it with our children by reading poetry, by enjoying art, by listening to music, by renewing old customs, by telling stories, by watching a ballet. It is a chance to grow with our children in an appreciation of all that is good, beautiful, true and real—a time to penetrate life and discover in it Jesus as the heart of the matter.

Any teaching about Advent also

needs to have a sense of the past. For Advent is a time for looking backward at the thousands of years before Jesus was born to learn how the people then dealt with uncertainty and unknowing. Advent united us with a whole chain of people longing for God's coming into their lives.

A blend of present and past can be achieved by introducing children to traditions that acquaint them with their Jewish ancestors and their Christian history. The particular blend and emphasis will necessarily vary according to age levels and particular circumstances. But the goal or aim, in all cases, is to encourage within ourselves and within each child a genuine expectancy of God's coming in daily experience as an expression of traditional Jewish and Christian spirituality.

To do that I have found some creative ways to involve ourselves and our children in the meaning of Advent. I'd like to share them with you.

THE ADVENT CALENDAR

There are two published versions of the Advent Calendar that I am familiar with. The Advent Box or Cube created by Sacred Design is the one that Thomas and Neil's family used so effectively. Its greatest value lies in its power to develop within a family's consciusness (or the consciousness of a class if used in school) a sensitivity to the coming of God in everyday things and in ordinary people. Alongside of the known, everyday things that are de-

scribed in terms of God's coming each day, the story of Jesus is also told. This calendar provides a marvelous blend of the present with the past. On the bottom of the cube is this description of Advent:

"Advent means coming,
God's coming to us,
Announced by an angel,
Proclaimed by a prophet,
Awaited by a family,
Accomplished in a stable.

Advent means Christ's coming

Into a waiting world,
Among ordinary needs and everyday
    experiences,
Along palm-strewn Jerusalem streets,
Amid fiery tongues on Pentecost
And again on the Last Day.

Advent means hurray!
For Christ's coming birthday
And his presence acknowledged in all
    the
Wonder-filled things around us.
We celebrate in his name
As we get ready for Christmas."

On the doors that are opened each
day, the ordinary is named and described and a Scripture passage is
cited. For example, on the sixth day,
God is described as coming "in our
family relationships, loving parents
and being brothers and sisters in
Christ—Ephesians 3:14-19."

If the Advent ceremony is conducted
at breakfast time as it was in Thomas
and Neil's home, it can become the
morning prayer. The passage from
Scripture can be read by different
members of the family. Perhaps an
Advent song could be sung. The ceremony can be both brief and simple.
What is important throughout the
day is to be alert to God's presence—
for example, on the sixth day, to his
presence in members of the family.
On other days the alertness to God's
presence might be as he is present in
nature, in smells, in fun, and, finally,
on Christmas day as he is present in
a child of humble beginnings called
Emmanuel, God-with-us for all time.

The other Advent Calendar that I'm

familiar with is the "Advent Chain of
Stars." It is published in book form
by Augsburg Press with the material
for the stars that represent the story
for each day attached to the inside
back cover. This is how Herbert
Martin, in the foreword of his book,
described his "Advent of Stars":

"On the first Sunday in Advent a few
years ago, my four children stood before a chain of stars which I had
hung on the wall according to an old
custom. After painstakingly counting
the stars, they asked, 'Dad, will you
tell us the story of the stars each
day?' So I decided to tell them and
other children the biblical message of
Advent as it is shown in the stars. In
doing this, I revive an old Advent
custom. Even though there are almost too many Advent traditions
today, most are not understood as visual symbols of Advent, of the coming of Jesus. Many popular customs
of Advent are too empty for children
and most devotions are above their
heads and therefore boring. But this
book combines Advent customs and
the Advent message. Isn't this the se-
cret desire of our children?—'Dad,
tell us the story of the stars.' "

In the pages of this little book the
stories and pictures of each week
form a unit. Each week speaks in its
special way of Advent, of the coming
of Jesus. The texts draw upon the ancient Advent traditions of the
Church. The continuous story is interrupted in the fourth week so that
you can break the chain anytime,
since Christmas falls on different
days of the week. For that week, pro-

phecies from the Old Testament serve as biblical texts.

The first week is entitled "Advent to the World" and explores Jesus' entry into Jerusalem. The promises of Jesus' return at the end of the world are considered in the second week, "Advent of the King." The third week, "Advent for the Heart," calls for openness to Jesus' coming. Finally, the fourth week, "Advent in the Light," leads directly to the manger. There are four big pictures for the four Sundays in Advent: the Annunciation, Mary and Elizabeth, Mary and Joseph on their journey to Bethlehem, and the birth in the stable. The enclosed instruction sheet contains ample directions for making the chain of stars.

Herbert Martin makes an important comment about the use of his booklet: "The child must sense that we adults also are gripped by the message of Advent. Only if we have grasped its meaning can we tell it honestly, soberly, and with joy." He suggests that parents and children try to pick the right time—perhaps after dinner when the whole family is gathered. He describes how his family celebrates: "When we have sung the Advent hymn we look at the picture and let the children ask questions till they are inwardly prepared to listen to the Bible text and the story of the star. Now we ask no more questions. Everybody listens and concludes by praying the Advent prayer, which like the hymn is printed at the beginning of each week."

The Advent calendar of stars, like the Advent Cube, imaginatively blends what the children experience in their lives with the story of the coming of Christ.

A family I know who use the calendar or chain of stars as a meaningful way of celebrating the meaning of Advent told me that they do not make stars out of the pictures and numbers, as is suggested. Instead they cut them out and slip them into pockets on a simple wall hanging that the mother designed. In this way the pieces remain in good condition and can be used over and over.

The Advent calendars described above could be adapted and used in a variety of creative ways. The single adult like myself can live out the Advent time according to a calendar made out of boxes. Last Advent I was living alone. Very early I found myself wanting to do something that would involve others as well as myself during each of the days of the season. An idea occurred to me, and since the experience was such a good one, I want to share it.

On a flat surface I placed twenty-four boxes and dated them. A carefully selected gift for the members of a needy family that I know was wrapped and placed in the box that corresponded with each day. The children I was teaching were told about my Advent calendar, and they, at times, helped me decide on appropriate gifts. If they wished, they could add gifts of their own and some of them did. Or, as happened in two cases, they initiated the custom in

surprise, but it was a great surprise, nonetheless.

Jesus came to us as a gift and he comes to us today in gifts. We can bring him to others in the gifts that we prepare and give.

Not in quite the same way as I carried out the theme of giving, but in much the same spirit, one of the sisters in my class this summer at St. Michael's College in Winooski, Vermont told what her community did one year during Advent. Instead of buying gifts for each other, they, through the St. Vincent de Paul Society, adopted a needy family. Each secretly bought a gift for each member of the family. On the Sunday before Christmas when they ordinarily exchanged the gifts they were giving to each other, they brought out the gifts they were giving to the family, enjoyed looking at and talking about them, and then wrapped them and put them under their tree. On Christmas Eve two of them went with a member of the St. Vincent de Paul Society to give the gifts and to wish their adopted family a merry Christmas.

THE ADVENT WREATH

More traditional, perhaps, and probably more familiar to most of us than the Advent calendar is the Advent Wreath. I mention it in this article because I believe that it should not be overlooked as a possibility for teaching about and celebrating the season. An experience that I had three years

their own families and prepared a surprise Christmas for a family that the St. Vincent de Paul Society knew about and selected. An official from the Society told the receiving families beforehand so it was not a complete ago led me to believe this way. At that time I was teaching religion on a once-a-week basis to one of two classes of sixth graders. An older man was teaching the other sixth grade class. On the first Sunday of Advent, he involved his group in putting an Advent Wreath together. They spent the class discussing its meaning as they were putting it together. Near the end of class they lit the first candle, said a prayer over the wreath, and sang, "O Come, O Come, Emmanuel."

All that I did with my group on that very same Sunday was teach an ordinary class and, at the end, I talked a bit about the season with them.

Somehow during the following week some of my sixth graders mingled with his sixth graders who told them about their Advent Wreath ceremony. On the following Sunday, my sixth graders begged to have an Advent Wreath and to do what had been done in the other classes.

I was chagrined and felt genuinely bad that I had failed to meaningfully involve my group in an experience that is part of our tradition, and which for them was an attractive way to enter into the season. The Advent Wreath symbolically unites our expectancy of Jesus' coming with that of millions of believers before us.

THE JESSE TREE

Advent, as we mentioned earlier, has deep roots in the past as well as the

present. The roots of the past are deeply Jewish. The use of a Jesse tree to celebrate Advent brings to light our Jewish ancestors and makes it possible for us to share in their hoping, their waiting and their longing for the promised Messiah, the promised Savior. A real tree might be used or a large construction paper tree, having on it twenty-five pieces that open or having with it twenty-five pieces that can be attached to it as the days of the season unfold. Printed on each piece is the name of a character having to do with preparing the way for Christ, or a quotation from Scripture, or a suitable symbol pertaining to the message for that particular day. Some of the people introduced as our and Jesus' ancestors are Adam and Eve, Noah, Abraham, Jacob, Moses, Jesse, David, John the Baptist, St. Joseph and Mary.

The Jesse tree is inspired by Isaiah's prophetic words, interpreted as referring to the coming of Jesus: "A shoot shall sprout from the stump of Jesse" (Is. 11:1).

These are some helpful ways of guiding children at home or in school through the Christian season of Advent. There are others as well. You may find further suggestions in the bibliography included with this article.

In closing I must admit that the greatest insight into the real meaning of Advent came from young Thomas and Neil and their Advent Box. Advent is a time of joining centuries of believing people who worked at a childlike awareness of God's coming into daily experience. Young Thomas says it all: "God comes to us in people. Janaan, you're a people." "God comes to us in a new day. This is a new day, isn't it?"

BIBLIOGRAPHY:

Advent Cube. Sacred Design, Minneapolis, Minnesota, 1971.

Anderson, Georgene and Raymond. *The Jesse Tree*. Philadelphia: Fortress Press, 1966.

Dallen, Rev. James. *Liturgical Celebration: Patterns for Advent and Christmas*. Cincinnati, Ohio: North American Liturgy Resources, 1974.

Haas, James E. *Shout Hooray!* New York: Morehouse-Barlow Co., 1972.

Haas, James E. and Lynne M. Haas. *Make a Joyful Noise*. New York: Morehouse-Barlow Co., 1973.

Heyer, Robert, Jean Marie Heisberger and Bernadette Kenny. *Let Us Pray 3: Resources for Celebrating*, New York: Paulist Press, 1972.

Huck, Gabe and Virginia Sloyan. *Children's Liturgies*. The Liturgical Conference, Washington, D.C., 1970.

Jamison, Andrew. *Liturgies for Children*. Cincinnati, Ohio: St. Anthony Messenger Press, 1975.

Konzelman, Robert. *The Talking Christmas Tree*. Minneapolis, Minnesota: Augsburg Publishing House, 1966.

Larsen, Ernest, C.SS.R. and Patricia Galvin. *Liturgy Begins at Home*. Liguori, Missouri: Liguori Publications, 1973.

LeBlanc, Etienne and Sister Mary Rose Talbot. *How Green Is Green?* Notre Dame, Indiana: Ave Maria Press.

Martin, Herbert. *Advent Chain of Stars*. Minneapolis, Minnesota: Augsburg Publishing House, 1968.

Morrison, Eleanor S. and Truman A. *Growing Up in the Family*. Philadelphia: United Church Press, 1964.

Rabalais, Sister Maria and Rev. Howard Hall. *Children Celebrate! Resources For Youth Liturgy*. New York: Paulist Press, 1974.

Sloyan, Virginia and Gabe Huck. *Parishes and Families*. The Liturgical Conference, Washington, D.C., 1973.

Catechist, November 1968, 1973, 1974. Pflaum/Standard, Dayton, Ohio. *Religion Teacher's Journal*, Nov./Dec. 1972 and 1974, February 1974. Twenty-Third Publications, Mystic, Connecticut.

PUBLIC TESTIMONY TO HOPE

Proclaiming the Lord till He Comes

Edward Kilmartin

A common characteristic of the exercise of faith in the New Testament period is the public testimony to hope. The author of 1 Peter exhorts Christians "to make a defense to anyone who calls you to account for the hope that is in you" (3:15). This hope was based on faith that Christ was present as the risen Lord in the baptized Christian (3:15, 18, 21). This hope looked to the promised fulfillment of God's activity through the presence of the Kyrios in the believer. At the same time it recognized that this activity would come to fruition in the measure that men were prepared to change their lives (Mk. 1:15) and to look for the "Kingdom of God and his righteousness" (Mt. 6:33). This hope, therefore, resulted in action because faith in God's activity through the risen Christ affected the whole of the believer's existence.

The experience of the action of the Spirit of Christ in Christians themselves and through them in others

Edward Kilmartin, S.J., is a professor of theology at Notre Dame. He writes frequently for *Theological Studies* in the area of sacramental theology.

who came to believe led to the recognition that what was done in faith had meaning for the furthering of the Kingdom of God. The New Testament does not accept a passive waiting for the advent of the Kingdom of God. In one way or another New Testament texts stress the importance of the works of faith as witness to the efficacious presence of God to mankind in Jesus Christ and so as a source of hope for the coming fulfillment of the unity of mankind in God. The Christian is viewed as responsible for exercising these works in order that mankind may find credible the Christian message of what God is doing now in history. According to 1 Peter it is the witness of a life conformed to the Gospel of Jesus (2:12a), the exercise of the priesthood of believers (2:9), which will lead the Gentiles to faith (2:12b). Paul points out the importance of "faith working through love" (Gal. 5:6). The Gospel of John makes love of the neighbor an explicit condition for discipleship (15:12). The Epistle of James calls for the patient "proving of faith in the works of love" (2:26; 5:7ff.).

However the goal of these works of faith is not merely the preaching of what God is doing now among the believers. These works are understood as having meaning for the realization of the Kingdom in its fullness. They lead others to participate in the Kingdom of God now: in God's activity through Christ which is the beginning of the final process of fulfillment that cannot be reversed. These works are viewed as a contribution to the realization of the Kingdom, for they further the unity of the human community in Christ. The New Testament does not speak of a complete discontinuity between what is happening now in the works of faith and the future fulfillment. The one God acts now through Christ in the works of faith and will bring the future fulfillment not independently of what the believer does now in faith. God is not seen as depriving mankind of responsibility for history. Rather he gives men the courage to act in history because he wants to save men in history.

It is true that, in the course of history of the faith, the interpretation of the concrete responsibility of Christians in history has varied. But at all stages of that history Christian faith has proclaimed the truth that man has the ability to give meaning to history because he has received meaning from God.

The works of faith are a contribution to the realization of the Kingdom of God because they are the proclamation of the effective presence of the Kingdom of God in the world. They can also be called a proclamation of the death of Christ: the victorious death which reveals itself in the effects it has on believers and through them on the world.

The eucharistic celebration of the New Testament communities centered on the victorious death of the Lord, his presence in the community, and the communion of the members with the risen Lord which is a foretaste of the heavenly banquet. In this context it would not be surprising if the early communities referred to the works of faith which show forth the victory of Christ and contribute to the fulfillment of that victory.

The eschatological saying of Mark 14:25 links the account of institution of the Eucharist to Jesus' expectation of the heavenly banquet of the Kingdom. The parallel passage in Matthew 26:29 indicates that the disciples will share this banquet with Jesus. This presentation reflects the implications drawn by the community from the absence of the Lord in the flesh and his presence in the Spirit. The community finds itself unfulfilled but surely ordered to the Kingdom where it will share in the glory of the Lord.

In the context of the account of institution of the Eucharist, Luke 22:15-18 [19-20], 21-38 draws out the implications of the absence of the Lord in the flesh for the situation in which Christians find themselves in the world. Here the account of institution is enclosed within a farewell address of Jesus which reflects a literary form of farewell address known in Judaism and which shows how the community interpreted its situation in view of Jesus' redemptive work, his absence in the flesh and his future coming in glory.

In this address Jesus describes what the community will experience when he has departed. This highlights the fact that the presence of the Lord in the eucharistic community is the presence of the absent one—absent in the flesh—who offered himself for the salvation of the world. The address contains the following elements: Jesus looks to his imminent death, predicting that he will not celebrate the Passover until the real-ization of the Kingdom of God (15-18). The community, however, will be united through the rite of the bread and cup to the absent one who gives himself as servant (19-20). The betrayal is mentioned which prepares the way for Jesus' death (21-23). Then Jesus instructs the Twelve to serve as he served (24-27) and promises the reward of fulfillment under the image of table-fellowship of Jesus with the community (28-30). After this he alludes to the dispersion of the disciples and the regrouping effected by Peter who is confirmed in his faith by Jesus' prayer (31-34). Finally he also predicts his death as fulfillment of Scripture and the strife which will be the lot of the disciples after his death (35-38).

This tradition reflects the community's understanding of its life with the risen Lord. In the absence of Jesus (15-18) the community, united through the rite of the bread and cup to the absent one who has given himself as servant for the salvation of the world (19-20), is a brotherhood which cannot abide a betrayer (21-23) and has a legacy of service (24-27). Though ordered to the heavenly banquet (28-30) it must undergo strife now (35-38). However it is assured the support of the absent one who strengthens Peter and, through the faithful disciple, supports the community (31-32).

From this text we can conclude that the true eucharistic community is one that accepts the call to proclaim the victorious death of Christ by living a life committed to that service which proclaims and furthers the progress of the fulfillment of the Kingdom until the coming of the Lord in glory. This conclusion is explicitly drawn by Paul where he considers the relationship of the Eucharist to Christian life.

In 1 Corinthians 10:1-13 Paul establishes a relationship between eucharistic communion and the Gospel. He insists that sharing in the "spiritual food and drink" (3-4) does not absolve one from following the Gospel of Jesus (5-13). In 1 Corinthians 10:14-33 he approaches the concrete problem of scandal given to the uninformed by the knowledgeable who eat meat derived from pagan sacrificial rites. In his view the unity of the eucharistic community in the one Lord demands conformity to the will of the Lord: seeking the neighbor's good and so not being the occasion of scandal for Jew, Greek or the Church of God. Finally, in 1 Corinthians 11:17-33 Paul calls attention to the ethical demands made on the community in the eucharistic celebration itself.

After the recitation of the account of institution of the Eucharist (23-25), Paul states: "For as often as you eat this bread and drink the cup you proclaim the Lord's death until he comes" (26). Paul thus situates this proclamation of the death of the Lord in the context of eating and drinking the eucharistic bread and cup. But it is not immediately clear how the eating and drinking become a proclamation of the death of the Lord. Does Paul know of two ways of proclaiming the death of the Lord:

(1) by the eucharistic words and actions which recall the redemptive work of Christ for us; (2) by the works of faith? Is Paul contrasting, in this pericope, the objective proclamation of the death of the Lord through the rite of the bread and cup with the conduct of the Corinthian community which tolerates cliques and so does not preach the death of Christ by works of faith? An interpretation of this sort does not correspond to Paul's view of things. It supposes a clear distinction between a valid and fruitful Eucharist. Such a distinction is foreign to Paul. Thus he is able to say without qualification: "When you meet together (understood: as you are accustomed to do), it is not the Lord's supper that you eat" (20). For Paul the outward accomplishment of the liturgical memorial is not sufficient to realize the Lord's supper.

Moreover the whole context of this pericope leads us to conclude that Paul is talking about what happens through the eating and drinking when those participating are living in union with God and their brothers and sisters. In such a situation they obtain a deeper share in the life of faith which makes possible more intimate union with God and loving service of the brethren.

The cup formula of the Pauline account of institution states: "This cup is the new covenant in my blood" (25). It announces that the drinking of the cup gives a share in a new covenant made possible by Jesus' death. The phrase "new covenant" relates

the gift of the Eucharist to the covenant proclaimed by Jeremiah 31:33 as being "written in the heart." It gives the gift of true knowledge and the power to live in a proper relationship with God and fellow men.

When Paul says: "you proclaim the death," he is talking about a proclamation of Jesus' death as redemptive. This proclamation takes place ultimately not through a mere word or action but through the visible effects which Jesus' victorious death has on the community of believers. In the measure that the community lives in union with one another, it is a concrete proclamation of the victorious death of Christ. The members show

by their lives that Christ's death is redemptive now, that it already heals the divisions of mankind brought about by sin.

Paul is talking about the ideal Eucharist in 1 Corinthians 11:26—the Eucharist in which the community dies to selfishness and lives for God and the brethren and so proclaims the death of the Lord. But this statement is meant as a challenge to the community of Corinth. Equivalently Paul says to them: You ought to proclaim the death of the Lord when you eat the bread and drink the cup.

It should be recalled that Paul is criticizing the conduct of the Corinthians at the Lord's supper in this passage (17-20). In view of this he does not hesitate to say: "It is not the Lord's supper that you eat" (20). The unworthiness mentioned in verse 27, which makes a mockery of the Eucharist, derives from the personal failure of the community to proclaim the victorious death of the Lord by dying to selfishness at the meal of the Lord. It is a sin against Christ who died for many and so gives mankind the means of living a life of love for one another.

To remedy this situation Paul calls for a "discerning of the body" (29). This means either (1) recognizing the eucharistic body in its claim to fraternal love, or (2) recognizing the meaning of the eucharistic and ecclesial body. This should lead to self-judgment and so a proper attitude for participation in the Lord's supper. Thus Paul concludes his advice: "Let a man examine himself and so eat the bread and drink the cup" (28).

In this passage Paul is concerned that the Eucharist be celebrated in such a way that it really proclaims the death of the Lord and so serves to build up the community in view of the second coming of the Lord.

The works of love which Paul demands for the proper celebration of the Eucharist have value for the growth of the kingdom, for they liberate those who do them from self-preoccupation and liberate those who are the recipients of these works from self-doubt.

In the measure that man in unliberated from self he is without hope. He is doomed to seek an answer to the meaning of his life which he cannot give himself. He needs a call to freedom. This call comes from the love of another which embraces him, acknowledges him as someone, and makes him courageous with regard to himself and his possibilities.

The call to freedom, of which Paul speaks in Galatians 5:13, originates from the love of Christ on the cross. Whoever hears and receives this call is freed from the flesh, i.e., from the compulsion always and everywhere to serve self. However Paul warns the liberated man: "Do not use your freedom as an opportunity for the flesh" (ibid.). To forestall this threat Paul gives this advice: "Through love be servants of one another" (ibid.). In Paul's view, through this service of love self-love will disappear and its opposite, self-hatred, will become superfluous. Moreover this service of love will have the effect of liberating the other from anxiety about self, self-doubt, etc. The love of the believers for one another liberates. Freedom is thus found in the community of love, of mutual service, of mutual recognition and joy in one another. In this freedom the Christian is able to enter into the world and serve to change it in view of the second coming of the Lord.

These reflections on the proclaiming of the Lord by the works of faith lead us up to the question: What should be the style of exercise of love today in a Christian community which celebrates the Eucharist together? What is required in our situation in order that the conduct of the community be a truly liberating force which promotes the development of the Kingdom of God until the Lord comes?

Here we can only allude to the answer that Christians must give to the challenge of pluralism which characterizes our period of history.

The sum total of experiences, insights, impulses and human possibilities in all spheres of human living is so immense and complex that it cannot be organized and reduced to a single integrated system. Hence there is no one representative of this total complex which can exercise authoritative control over all the elements. All these elements are factors in modern man's picture of the world, and in his interpretation of himself, which in turn constitutes the situation in which he lives out his life. They cause a change in the concrete form which the life of faith takes.

Within the Christian community this pluralism exists, and necessarily so, because of the intimate connection between faith and life. Faced with this pluralism which tends to separate members of a community, dialogue is required if Christians are to live together. Here we are talking about communication between persons as subjects of feeling, thoughts and achievements. These interpersonal relations tend to the development of the human person and society, relations of understanding and truth, of love and peace, of encounter and

communion, of hope and fulfillment.

Granting the necessity of pluralism in the Christian community and the necessity of dialogue to ascertain whether what we think and do is consistent with a common confession of faith and for mutual growth in personhood, it becomes apparent that a new style of exercise of love is required.

It must be a love which takes for granted that unity does not necessarily imply unanimity among members: human solidarity on all levels. Such a love takes for granted that the death of the Lord is proclaimed, in spite of the existence of many human differences in a community, by its power to unite all men and women of good will. This love will not instinctively look for the deepest experience and most telling proclamation of the death of the Lord in the gathering of like-minded persons romantically involved, but rather where the pious and liberal, the weak and strong (to use Paul's expression) jostle against one another yet still confess the same faith and pray for one another.

It must be a love which aims at more than the acceptance of differences. Since this love has to do with acknowledgment of the other, with liberation of the other, it should strive for reconciliation. Such a love recognizes that it is not sufficient to resign oneself to the fact that unanimity without opposition cannot be obtained in history and so look beyond human differences to the point of reconciliation: Jesus Christ who unites all despite their differences. It accepts the message of the Fourth Gospel that the believer has the power in the Lord to love others "as I have loved you" (15:12), namely, "to the end" (of love) (13:12), to the choosing of the neighbor over self (10:17). This love knows that it can and must go through human differences in order to obtain that reconciliation which the Gospel demands. It knows that it is called to encounter the other, accept differences and aspire to further reconciliation and the communion which is already given in common faith in Jesus Christ.

Jesus contrasts his legacy of peace with the tribulation which Christians will have in the world (Jn. 14:27; 16:33). It is a peace in which the human heart is not torn between self-seeking and surrender to the will of God. It is a peace which can overcome our tribulations caused by our differences through the light of faith which recognizes that they do not ultimately define our relations to one another. Their relativity is judged in the light of our union with God in Christ.

A healthy ethic of conflicts does not run counter to the demands of Christian unity. Rather it is an ethic which considers all conflict as sinful: a childish representation of unity which misunderstands the importance and legitimacy of conflicts. A deeper understanding of unity in Christ which assumes conflicts, pluralism and a corresponding ethic is needed especially today. It is a pre-condition for the confession of our unity in Christ with our lips and our hearts and in our daily contact with one another. It is a pre-condition for the celebration of the ideal Eucharist which truly proclaims, in the Pauline sense, the victorious, liberating death of Christ until he comes.

ADULT EDUCATION PROGRAM

by Sara and Richard Reichert

GENERAL INTRODUCTION

The purpose of this educational supplement is to provide a practical plan for adult religious education. This plan will be based on selected articles from each issue of NEW CATHOLIC WORLD and will provide adult education programs for eight weeks.

Each session will be built upon key articles and will explode outward from these experiences, information, and group techniques.

The NEW CATHOLIC WORLD ADULT EDUCATION PROGRAM provides:

—continuous preplanned adult education program
—rich range of topics
—short-term commitment
—CCD teacher-enrichment program
—probing content-articles on today's issues integrated with experience-centered educational plans
—educational tools that are practical and spark interest

The creation of a climate conducive to learning is very important. A proper climate in an educational setting should help people be at ease and should stimulate sharing as well as personal activity. Clear, concise directions and careful preparation will facilitate this. Therefore:

—the director should prepare carefully beforehand.
—participants should have read the related articles.
—if a series of directions are given the director should wait until one stage is completed before announcing the next stage.
—the purpose of each session as well as its relation to the whole should be explained.

I. FIRST WEEK PROGRAM (90 Minutes)

HOW MANY MILES TO BETHLEHEM?

A. INTRODUCTION
—AIM: to more meaningfully celebrate the birth of Christ participants will learn and experience one or more Christmas customs which have developed in different lands.
—Participants should have read Mary Louis Tietjen's article.
—Materials: Supplies will vary from group to group or parish to parish.

B. EDUCATIONAL PLAN
(90 minutes)
1. This whole session will be spent preparing for the fair.
2. Well before Dec. 25th but into the

Advent Season participants will sponsor a Christmas Fair as elaborate or as simple as the imagination and creativity of the participants allow.

3. The actual fair would consist of an afternoon or evening during which there might be:
—booths of native food, gifts, and apparel
—plays or shows consisting of songs, dances, etc. of native customs and songs done by the grade school children and/or youth
—an evening of native culinary delights
—games of native children.

4. The preparation would be a learning experience that would:
—begin with research (suggested titles at end of article)
—choosing the one or many nationalities from which the Christmas customs would flow
—involve setting up committees
—purchasing supplies
—assigning tasks
—making the items and preparing the skits

5. N.B. This type of event can bring a parish together forming a community which creates a basis for the Eucharist and simultaneously be a fund raising event for a sagging treasury.

....

The above plan will not be suitable for some parishes, so the following alternative is given.
(10 mins.)

1. The director explains to the group the purpose of the session stressing the need and beauty of developing and carrying on customs as a nation, community and family. The director then divides up the participants into groups of four or five appointing a secretary for each group.
(40 mins.)

2. The participants are to:
—determine what a custom is; i.e., define what their particular group will mean by the term "custom"
—give examples of customs in their experience of Christmas
—evaluate the value of these customs, i.e. should they be handed down from generation to generation, do they convey the true message of Christmas, etc.?
—give examples of customs they would like to see introduced into their families or communities.
(30 mins.)

3. Share these customs with the entire group and discuss concrete ways that these customs can be introduced into a family
(10 mins.)

4. Use Mary's Magnificat (Luke 1:46-55) as a closing prayer with sides alternating each verse. One or all of the "O Antiphons" (cf. article by C. J. McNapsy) could be recited as a chorus after each verse.

II. SECOND WEEK PROGRAM (90 Minutes) HOW TO CELEBRATE THE FOUR SUNDAYS OF ADVENT IN A PARISH

A. INTRODUCTION
—AIM: to develop a deeper and more prayerful liturgy by growing in an awareness of the basic elements necessary for a Eucharistic celebration.
—Participants should have read Charles Gusmer's article.
—Materials: copies of Charles Gusmer's article, blackboard and chalk.

B. EDUCATIONAL PLAN
(10 mins.)
1. The director explains to the participants that this session is designed to draw from them two or three weak areas in their liturgy which as a group they might strengthen. The participants are divided into groups of four or five with one person designated as secretary.
(30 mins.)
2. Each group using Gusmer's article and points of "Evaluation of Present Liturgical Services" draws up a list of *three* specific areas where the parish's liturgy could be improved. After the area is identified the group should list one positive and practical recommendation for improving that area.
(5 mins.)
3. The secretary lists on the blackboard the three areas and recommendations of each group.
(30 mins.)
4. The director asks the group to arrive at a consensus of three specific recommendations from all the groups and sets up committees who are responsible for implementing by a specific time each recommendation.
(15 mins.)
5. The group closes their session with an Advent para-liturgical celebration prepared ahead of time. Suggested readings and songs are in every parish missalette.

III. THIRD WEEK PROGRAM (90 Minutes) CHRISTMAS SEASON FAMILY CELEBRATIONS

A. INTRODUCTION
—AIM: to help participants experience and understand the meaning of hopeful waiting.
—Participants should have read John Gallen's article.
—Materials: a pan of water, 12 marbles, coins or pebbles.

B. EDUCATIONAL PLAN
(5 mins.)
1. Seat participants in a semi-circle in front of a table on which has been placed a pan of water. Ask for silence. Then instruct them that their task will be to listen intently, eyes closed, to see if they can count how

many marbles (coins, pebbles) are dropped into the pan in a five minute period. Demonstrate once, allowing them to keep eyes open, to insure that all can hear the splash.
(5 mins.)

2. Once the exercise begins, the instructor drops marbles at random intervals during the five minute period. Note that the exercise should last at least five minutes to create a sensation of waiting. The instructor should drop marbles one at a time. Actual number dropped is up to instructor. (E.g., all, two or three, only one.)
(5 mins.)

3. At the end of the five minutes, ask participants to say how many they counted. Then tell them correct number. (Accuracy of participants has no direct bearing on purpose of exercise.)
(5 mins.)

4. Next solicit comments with some of following questions:
—Was activity a "strain"? Did you find yourself getting impatient? Why? Why not?
—Does anticipation cause you to *hear* better? Make you more alert? Make your ears play tricks on you?
—Does the "waiting" make time go slower or faster?
—Can you think of situations in real life where you have had to wait in-
tently? Describe them.
(20 mins.)

5. Instructor should summarize observations about nature of waiting: intensity, attentiveness, need for "silence" etc. and then review the main points of Gallen's article regarding Advent as a period of waiting.

6. Divide participants into groups of six or eight and ask the central idea of the article: God is already with us so we can wait hopefully for our salvation to fully appear. These questions can provide the framework:
—What are come signs that God is already present in our lives?
—What does hopeful waiting entail?
—What is the salvation we are awaiting?
(30 mins.)

7. Using the readings for next Sunday's liturgy together with appropriate Advent hymns, develop a prayer service along the following lines:
Hymn, 1st Reading, reflection, Spontaneous prayer (optional), Hymn, 2nd Reading, reflection, Spontaneous prayer or a Collect by Instructor, Hymn, 3rd Reading, reflection, Closing prayer and hymn.
Service should be slow paced and reflective but not heavy—creating a mood of hopeful waiting.

IV. FOURTH WEEK PROGRAM (90 Minutes)
NOW WE WATCH FOR THE DAY

A. INTRODUCTION
—AIM: To teach us how to make Christmas a season of celebrations
rather than a day or few moments.
—Participants should have read Gabe Huck's article.

—Materials: paper and pencils, dupli-
cating machine and copies of Gabe
Huck's article.

B. EDUCATIONAL PLAN

(15 mins.)

1. The director explains to the group
that they are a nucleus who will help
the entire community learn to celebrate the season of Christmas by
making it a series of celebrations
for all members of the community
over a period of days.

(N.B. As other articles have discussed
ways of preparing for Christmas the
session will devote its time and purpose
to celebrating the season of Christmas
after Dec. 25th.) The director will divide the participants into groups of
four or five and give them the following format to follow:

—list all the means of celebrating the
days after Christmas that they are
familiar with and those which have
seemed "to work" for them.
—list all the people who could and
should be included in the celebration remembering a) all ages b) the
poor c) the shut-ins.
—enumerate the days and feasts after
Christmas as suggested in the article
with a possible celebration: e.g. Dec.
26th feast of St. Stephen: visit someone in the neighborhood whom
others and themselves have social-
ly "persecuted".

(45 mins.)

2. The participants will work through
the format given with the secretary keeping notes.

(15 mins.)

3. The participants assemble as a big
group and decide the means by
which they might make their find-
ings available to the whole parish.
One alternative might be a supplement to the Sunday bulletin.

(15 mins.)

4. The group closes its session with a
song or demonstration prepared
ahead of time by a group of one
such celebration that all might experience after Christmas. E.g., pass
out various blessings for wine to be
used on Dec. 27th and have a toast
to St. John.

V. FIFTH WEEK PROGRAM (90 Minutes)
BETWIXT AND BETWEEN

A. INTRODUCTION

—AIM: to help participants appreciate
that Advent is a "looking forward"
to what has "already happened".
—Participants should have read Ralph
A. Keifer's article.
—Materials: paper and pencils.

B. EDUCATIONAL PLAN

(10 mins.)

1. Ask each participant in groups of
six to eight to write down eight to
ten adjectives or descriptive words
for the Church's attitude toward
Advent and a parallel list of eight
to ten words that the "world"
might use to describe the same
period of the year.

(15 mins.)

2. Groups share results and then observe all instances where Church's

attitude and world's are similar (E.g. joyful) and where they are contradictory (E.g. penance vs. parties). Next have them observe where lists used to describe Church's attitude apparently contradicts self (E.g. joyful vs. penance)
(5 mins.)

3. Results of these comparisons could be placed on blackboard.
(20 mins.)

4. Having highlighted the "contradictions" in the Church's attitude about Advent, the instructor should review Keifer's article, centering on the fact that in Advent we are asked to rejoice in what has happened even while waiting for it to happen—namely Jesus' presence in our midst.

Summarize this review by saying the task of Advent is to discover Jesus already present even while longing for the full manifestation of his presence (parousia). Hence the joy vs. longing, the penance vs. rejoicing of Advent.

5. Now ask participants in their groups to attempt to identify ways in which Jesus is already present (basis for rejoicing) and ways in which his "appearance" is still lacking (basis for longing).
(5 mins.)

6. Groups should share results of discussion.
(15 mins.)

7. Ask each group to make up two short prayers—one expressing the joy of Advent, the other expressing the longing. These should be used as a basis for a brief closing prayer service.

VI. SIXTH WEEK PROGRAM (90 Minutes) TEACHING
CHILDREN TO CELEBRATE THE MEANING OF ADVENT

A. INTRODUCTION

—AIM: To become aware of the ways God is present to us each day to concretize this awareness by imaginatively creating an Advent calendar which renews and clarifies this awareness.

—Participants should have read Janaan Manternack.

—Materials: paper and pencils construction paper, scissors, glue, miscellaneous craft materials.

B. EDUCATIONAL PLAN
(15 mins.)

1. The director explains to the participants that:

—Advent is a time to become more aware of the ways in which Emmanuel is with us now in order to be ready to receive him in a fuller manner at Christmas.

and

—Often it is necessary for us to actually work through a project together in order to be less fearful of introducing it in our families when alone.

2. The participants *in twos* are asked to list as many ways as there are days of Advent (for 1975-25) in

which Christ is present to us here and now. Following ideas mentioned in Janaan Manternack's article they would be something like:
—God comes to us in people.
—God comes to us in a new day.

3. Once the list is drawn up, participants create an Advent calendar using any means they desire. The article suggests the box and the stars.

(60 mins.)

4. Participants draw up list and create Advent calendars.
(15 mins.)

5. Each set shares their projects with the group and mentions how they will use them including: time, participants and hopes for what this might achieve in their respective families.

VII. & VIII. SEVENTH AND EIGHTH WEEK PROGRAM (90 Minutes)

PROCLAIMING THE LORD UNTIL HE COMES

A. INTRODUCTION
—AIM: To seek to grasp *with faith* how to "Proclaim the Lord Until He Comes".
—Participants should have read Edward Kilmartin's article.

B. EDUCATIONAL PLAN
N.B. The theology presented in Kilmartin's article is so rich and well thought out that it merits two sessions of 90 mins. each. In this kind of situation it is advisable to use one session to allow the participants to read the article, jot down ideas and questions either alone or in groups and use the second session for a teaching or learning experience.

The theology in "Proclaiming the Lord Until He Comes" is comprehen-

sive not only of the whole Advent season but of the Christian life in general. It does not lend itself to dynamics, creative experiences or group discussion but would best be treated in one or other of the following formats:

1. After the participants have read and jotted down questions to this article, either the director or a trained catechist would present the main concepts using diagrams, discussion and questions and answers.

or

2. Each group of three or four would be responsible for the material in "x" number of paragraphs or pages and of presenting it to the entire group through whatever means they feel comfortable.